THE POWER OF POSITIVE HORSE TRAINING

Also by Sarah Blanchard from Howell Book House:

Carriage Driving: A Logical Approach Through Dressage Training (with Heike Bean)

THE POWER OF POSITIVE HORSE TRAINING

Saying Yes to Your Horse

Sarah Blanchard

Howell Book House
Published by Wiley Publishing, Inc., Hoboken, New Jersey

For general information on our other products and services or to obtain technical support please contact our Customer Care Department within the U.S. at (800) 762-2974, outside the U.S. at (317) 572-3993 or fax (317) 572-4002.

Wiley also publishes its books in a variety of electronic formats. Some content that appears in print may not be available in electronic books. For more information about Wiley products, please visit our Website at www.wiley.com.

Library of Congress Cataloging-in-Publication Data:

Blanchard, Sarah.
  The power of positive horse training : saying yes to your horse / Sarah Blanchard.—1st ed.
    p. cm.
  Includes bibliographical references and index.
  ISBN-13: 978-0-7645-7819-9 (pbk.)
  ISBN-10: 0-7645-7819-7 (pbk.)
  1. Horses—Training. 2. Human-animal communication. I. Title.
  SF287.B596 2005
  636.1'0835—dc22
                  2004025768

Printed in the United States of America

10 9 8 7 6 5 4 3 2 1

Book design by Lissa Auciello-Brogan
Cover design by Jose Almaguer
Book production by Wiley Publishing, Inc. Composition Services

CONTENTS

FOREWORD

We all, over the years, develop our personal philosophies about the areas that are important in our lives. If you are a horseman, you have a philosophy about working with horses that arises from trial and error and learning from others, both human and equine. One of life's joys is to meet someone who shares your beliefs, so that your conversation is one of support and agreement and is uplifting for both. Sarah Blanchard is a writer who agrees with one of my most basic philosophies and has the knowledge and skill to expand upon it and make it more accessible to others.

Like so many horsemen of my age, I grew up in the "old" tradition of the master-slave relationship with the horse. "Don't be a passenger!" and "Don't let him get away with that!" were phrases that typify the attitude we were supposed to have. That, and the belief that the faster you could train a horse, the better trainer you were.

Over the years I found these ways of thinking more and more unsatisfactory, but it wasn't until I retired from active teaching that I really found the time to devote to following my instincts. Since that time I have been involved in long discussions on the Internet, delved into many books, attended clinics, and generally tried to increase my knowledge of what has come to be known as natural horsemanship but could just as well be called "practical horsemanship" because it works far better than the old methods. The underlying principle is that the horse becomes not a slave but a willing partner because we take the trouble to earn his trust and learn to understand his needs. Obviously, this is a tremendously complex subject. Horses come in many, many different sizes, shapes, and mentalities. Their reactions to us also depend to a great extent on their personal histories—a horse who has been abused is going to require totally different handling from one who has always been handled by sympathetic, intelligent trainers.

Therefore, when I am introduced to a new book that gives me new and greater insight into the world of understanding horses, I am excited and intrigued. Sarah and I go back a long way, since we both came from the same part of Connecticut and rode with the same instructor, though at different times. And Sarah has come a long way in her understanding of the most effective and compassionate ways of communicating with and getting the best results from horses. Her book is thorough, clearly written, and interesting in its approach and the areas it covers. It is a welcome addition to the literature in the field of horse training and should be in the library of any serious, caring horseman.

Gincy Self Bucklin
Narragansett, RI, November 2004
Author of *What Your Horse Wants You to Know* and
How Your Horse Wants You to Ride: Starting Out, Starting Over

ACKNOWLEDGMENTS

I want to thank first and foremost my non-horsey but always enthusiastic husband and most loyal supporter, Rich Valcourt. Rich has always cheered me on with his positive attitude and a willingness to walk dogs, cook dinner, and celebrate every milestone connected with this book. He has also happily offered his camera and his excellent photographer's eye to produce many of the photos in this book.

Heartfelt thanks go also to good friends Bird and Colin McIver, who have opened their hearts and their barn to me. The idea for this book first grew out of a discussion with Bird, and since that conversation she has generously shared with me her horses, her time, her dedication to learning, and her thoughtful insights about the nature of horses. Colin also shared his valuable time and professional photographer's expertise, which is much appreciated.

Thanks also to the students and friends who gave their time and brought their horses to ride for hours before the cameras: riders Meredith Acly, Lori Campbell, Lisa Johnston, Rachel Rechtman, Emily VanVleet Singer, and Holly Walsh; and horses Coosa Lani, Leo Bar Nani, Taser, Joe, and Willa. Emily also contributed some of her own top-notch photography for this book.

And a big Hawaiian *mahalo* goes to editor Beth Adelman and senior editor Roxane Cerda at Wiley Publishing for guiding me through the process from manuscript to publication.

PREFACE

Think of a typical schoolroom: The teacher explains the material and then the students ask questions and listen for the teacher's answers. The teacher asks questions, too, to check the students' comprehension, and provides feedback: "Good, that's right." "Yes, that's partly correct." "No, not quite. Let's look at this a different way."

But what would happen if the teacher *never* said yes to the students? What if the teacher corrected the wrong answers but simply ignored the right responses? How long would the students want to listen, and how much learning would take place?

Face it: If you own, train, or ride a horse, you are a teacher, whether or not you intended to be one. This is a constant learning experience for both of you, and you are your horse's primary partner in learning.

For four decades I've watched, learned from, coached, and worked with a wide variety of horses, riders, and other trainers—not just to win in shows or to make a profit but to find the satisfaction that comes from helping the horse and the human make the connection of trust and understanding. My goal is to help people and horses learn how to reach a level of successful teamwork that creates a sense of pure delight.

I also spent 15 years working in corporate management and marketing, where I discovered how important it is not only to provide confident leadership but also to understand underlying motivations so you can create a successful team. I also learned how a skilled communicator can turn every roadblock into an opportunity for success. So what does this have to do with horse training? The horse's natural instincts set the stage for effective teamwork, but we humans must understand his motivation and create a language based on requests, responses, and rewards—all delivered in the horse's own language. We need to understand how horses interact within the equine herd and then step into their world. Translating needs and expectations from human language to horse language—and back again—becomes easier when you understand the native culture.

This book doesn't cover every step in the process of training a green horse from the ground up. Instead, it focuses on communication skills and methods that trainers and riders need to master in order to facilitate successful, lifelong relationships with their horses. I don't cover halter training, ground driving, or ponying the young horse, for instance; but I do explain the importance of ground exercises and work on the longe because these involve skills and methods of communication that will benefit all horses and riders at almost all ages and nearly every stage of training.

Some people will call this a book about natural horsemanship, and others might say it looks suspiciously like a dressage book, although I've tried not to use either term too often. But natural horsemanship and dressage are essentially different branches of the same tree, so this book incorporates many principles and exercises from both. The goal, after all, is to create a trusting, willing, enjoyable team relationship with our horses, no matter what style we ride or what our individual goals might be. I hope it will find a wide audience with all riders and horse owners.

In some ways, training a horse is like bringing up a child. The most valuable gifts we can give to either a horse or a child are a good education, a long healthy life, and a positive attitude toward work. The skilled, well-mannered horse who displays a willingness to work will have value in the eyes of all the people who may enjoy riding or caring for him in the future. By giving that horse a good education, you're helping to ensure that he'll have a good life.

And, as my first riding instructor (my mother) always said, the best way to teach a horse (or a child) is to model the behavior you're seeking. Offer respect to earn respect. Communicate clearly and logically to get clear, logical feedback. Think carefully and deliberately to elicit careful, deliberate responses. Give more to get more back. Be a leader because every team needs a leader. And finally, it's the leader's responsibility to catch 'em being good, so you can reward, reward, reward.

Part I

THE NATURE OF POSITIVE TRAINING

1

WHY DO HORSES (USUALLY) DO WHAT WE TELL THEM?

ong before we rode horses, we hunted them, killed them, and ate them. In more recent times, we've developed elaborate methods to dominate them and make money from them. We've turned them into beasts of burden, starved them, beaten them, and sent them to war, even while glorifying the "noble horse" in songs, stories, and beautiful pictures. And in some cultures, we still eat them.

Given all this, it's rather remarkable that horses can ever learn to trust and willingly obey humans. Yet every foal is born curious, sociable, and trusting, ready to give his loyalty and obedience to a worthy leader, human or equine. From the horse's point of view, the most important questions in relation to his leader are very basic ones: What will happen to me? Will I have food, water, space to move around in, good friends to keep me safe? Whom should I trust?

From the human's point of view, the key questions we ask are also simple: Why shouldn't my horse step aside, pick up a foot, change leads, chase cows, cross a stream, jump, run, halt quietly, leave his friends, or walk into a trailer, just because I tell him to? But the questions we *should* ask are just the opposite: Why does my horse do any of these things willingly? What is his motivation? (In business parlance, the question would be, What's the customer's incentive?)

If you've never asked those questions, or if your quick answer is, "Because I'm the boss and I said so," then it's time to step back and think more carefully about the horse-human relationship from the horse's point of view. If your horse's obedience is the result of force and domination—not mutual trust, equine logic, and thoughtful understanding—you and your horse will never feel completely safe or comfortable with each other. And if a half-ton horse doesn't feel safe and secure, he's likely to choose one of his instinctive alternatives (run, fight, or resist), and someone may get hurt.

A Test of Trust

One day after a storm I was riding Star, my 6-year-old Thoroughbred-Appaloosa event horse, on the trails. The storm had brought down a large maple tree, and a section of heavy trunk lay about three and a half feet off the ground right across a flat section of my trail.

Although the upper branches of the tree were sprawled across the ground in a forbidding tangle to the left of the main trunk, the trail beneath it offered good, solid footing and a nice straight approach. All we had to do was jump clean through the middle section and we'd be fine. My horse was a bold cross-country jumper who'd tackled far more difficult obstacles on some tough New England courses. I was wearing my helmet, Star was wearing his protective galloping boots, and this nice, new cross-country obstacle was just begging to be jumped.

Our approach was straight, but perhaps I was the slightest bit unbalanced, or perhaps Star decided he could brush through the bushy tree branches instead of jumping the solid trunk. But the branches were not "brushable." He caught a front leg on an inflexible branch, and we somersaulted over the tree.

I found myself lying in the dirt on the far side of the tree, staring at the underside of Star's girth and the soles of his front feet. He'd flipped completely over and landed flat on his left side. Both of my legs, from mid-thigh down, were firmly wedged under his barrel. His front hooves were inches away from my right ear, and his hind feet were resting against my left shoulder. For a few stunned seconds, neither of us moved. Then my horse tried to rise, but he couldn't—my body, pinned beneath his, prevented him from rolling up onto his sternum and getting his legs under him. And I was stuck underneath him.

Four size-six horse hooves, complete with steel shoes and bell boots, were waving in the air just inches from my head.

With no real plan in mind, I grabbed a front foot in my right hand and a rear leg in my left and talked to him in a reassuring, authoritative voice. I have no idea what I said, but the tone must have been right because Star looked at me lying beneath his legs, heaved a big sigh, dropped his head, and lay quietly. He seemed to be saying, "Oh good, there's the boss, she'll know what to do." And for the next several minutes, while I developed a plan to get us untangled, he simply lay there and waited for directions.

That's negative horse training. Negative training ignores the horse's needs, desires, and logical thought processes. It creates resistance and provides the horse with no legitimate reason to cooperate, other than pain or the threat of pain.

Positive horse training, on the other hand, defines the horse-human relationship as a team, with reasonable motivations and logical rewards for cooperation. Positive horse training uses well-timed rewards to build trust and respect between horse and human. Trust and respect, after all, are two faces of the same coin; you can't have one without the other.

I decided the only way to get this big horse off of me was to use his legs as levers, roll him onto his saddle, and try to crawl out from underneath. I took a firm grip on two of his legs, front and back, and heaved him up onto his back. Star allowed himself to be rolled almost upside down, then settled back onto his side, legs outstretched. I scrambled backward, stood, and walked all around my still-prostrate horse, checking for injuries and reminding him with a quiet voice to remain still. Then I gave a gentle tug on the reins and said crisply, "Up, now." He rose and shook himself, and I led him slowly home, patting and talking and reminding him of what a wonderful horse he was. We were both stiff for a few days but otherwise uninjured.

What was so remarkable about this incident, aside from the fact that we were tremendously lucky not to break both our necks?

Simply this: Caught in a similar situation, the average horse would have descended into pure panic. The first instinct of a trapped prey animal is to struggle blindly, to get back onto his feet at whatever cost, and to flee to safety or to strike out if he can't get free. Nothing triggers a horse's survival instinct more than the feeling of being caught and unable to run away.

Why didn't Star panic? It wasn't as if we'd rehearsed that scenario. I'd never asked him to lie down or get up on command, and I'd certainly never trapped myself under his legs on purpose. He was certainly not dull or lethargic by nature, nor was he the most intelligent horse I've ever trained. Throughout his training, however, I'd always worked to develop his confidence in humans. I'd raised him, his dam, and his grand-dam from birth, and I'd spent countless hours encouraging their trust and helping them face and overcome their instinctive fears. Star's early training had included many carefully structured hours of low-threat combat training (see chapter 14), which introduces and then defuses many common fear triggers.

We had developed behavioral patterns for dealing with unexpected situations that required mutual trust and confidence. The habits of obedience and trust in both of us were strong enough to overcome instincts and fears. That's why we were both able to walk away from that fall.

And yes, we returned two weeks later and jumped that tree with a lot more focus and care. Star never hesitated but cleared it by at least a foot and a half.

Every Teacher Is a Learner, Every Learner Is a Teacher

You may not consider yourself a teacher or a horse trainer. But if you ride, drive, or handle a horse at even the most basic level of interaction, you are contributing to the horse's training. Horse trainers often refer to the early stages of training as "starting" a horse, but very few have the audacity to call any phase of training "finishing" the horse—because training is always dynamic and will therefore never be "finished." *Every* human-horse interaction—even something as routine as feeding, haltering, or grooming—does one of three things: It confirms, strengthens, or weakens the horse's trust and confidence in humans. It works the other way, too: Every horse-human interaction confirms, strengthens or weakens the human's trust and confidence in the horse. But since we humans are the ones who possess the larger brains and control the horse's environment, we're supposed to be in charge—so *we're* the ones who are responsible for figuring out how to make the relationship work.

You may not consider yourself a student—particularly if you haven't seen the inside of a classroom for a few decades. But the very best horsemen and horsewomen all know that every ride on every horse teaches us something new, if we simply listen and pay attention. Alois Podhajsky, the legendary and longtime director of the Spanish Riding School in Vienna, expresses this understanding very well in his book *My Horses, My Teachers.*

I have not written this book as a how-to manual for training horses from birth through the highest levels of success. (There are many good books and training systems already available, and I'll refer to several of them at various points.) Primarily, this book was written to encourage you—the concerned and

Emily Singer

The positive trainer builds confidence and establishes patterns of obedience by tapping into every horse's need for comfort, security, and trustworthy leadership.

committed horseperson in any discipline and at any skill level—to think more carefully about how humans communicate with horses and how they need to communicate with us. I want to help you create a logical, consistent system of request, response, and reward that will help you and your horse establish excellent teamwork. I'll provide you with a model for lesson plans that you can use to clarify the steps in reward-based training and adapt them to your own training program. I'll also give you a series of tried-and-true exercises to develop your balance, your communication skills, and your ability to say yes to your horse.

In other words, we're going to take a look at the communication process from the horse's point of view and understand how his behavior can be influenced so you can get what *you* want by giving him exactly what *he* needs and wants. That's positive horse training.

I can hear the protests: "But all my horse wants to do is loaf and hang out with his buddies!"

That may be true—and you've identified two of the horse's basic motivations—but it's not the whole truth. And you can use those desires (for security, relaxation, and companionship) as rewards that will work in your favor. If your training follows a consistent reward-based learning process, your horse will *want* to please you. After all, who do you want to have working with you? A friend who will trust your judgment in a scary situation, who will work extra hard just to make you happy? Or a stranger who grudgingly does what he's told, grabs his paycheck, goes on strike at every opportunity, and quits as soon as the work gets tough?

Another protest: "My horse will be spoiled if I'm too nice to him!"

This isn't about being nice or not nice; it's about trust, understanding, responsibility, respect, and logical consequences. You won't spoil your horse if, from his point of view, your requests and rewards are both logical and appropriate. With a deeper understanding of how to create trust by knowing what motivates your horse, you'll be able to view the horse's needs (his goals) as incentives for good performance (your goals).

Reward-based positive training uses both positive and negative reinforcement to help you accomplish what you want by giving your horse what he wants and needs. Negative reinforcement? Isn't that punishment, the opposite of reward? No, not at all. Let's review some basic terms in learning theory.

Patterns of Learning

How does learning occur? Behavioral scientists have identified four ways that most animals—including humans—learn a specific behavior. These four patterns of learning are positive reinforcement, negative reinforcement, punishment, and extinction. Both positive and negative reinforcement *strengthen* behavior by providing appropriate rewards for correct responses. Punishment and extinction *weaken* behavior because they do *not* provide rewards.

Positive Reinforcement

Positive reinforcement isn't just a reward for correct behavior; it's a specific pattern of learning that occurs when a particular behavior receives a reward. Here's what happens: A reward is offered, the horse uses trial and error to find the response required to receive the reward, and the horse gets the reward. The trainer repeats the offer-response-reward sequence, and the horse soon discards the behaviors that don't work, zeroes in on what does work, and shortens his response time to get the reward faster. The horse has learned something new by associating a reward with a previously unrelated action.

Perhaps the best-known example of positive reinforcement used in training is clicker training, which teaches an animal to obey commands by associating a food reward with the sound of a mechanical clicker. Clicker training was originally developed to train free-swimming dolphins, which obviously can't be pushed or pulled into a particular behavior. One of its great advantages is that the animal initiates the actions that result in a reward. If training sessions are scheduled around feeding times, this method can produce rapid results because the animal is hungry. (Food rewards are discussed further in chapter 3.)

Pure positive reinforcement doesn't work in all training situations. It's a trial-and-error process that requires a lot of time and patience because the horse has to initiate the behavior that yields a reward. It does work well, however, in situations where you have little or no physical control over the horse (for example, when you want your horse to come when called). It's easy to train a horse to come when you call or whistle, but it's amazing how few horse owners bother to teach this. Most people trudge out into the field, walk up to the grazing horse, and hope he doesn't leave while they're buckling on the halter. But if every time you enter the paddock you offer a reward, connect a certain signal (a call or whistle) with the reward, and use the signal to *catch the horse being good* when he takes even a single step toward you, you'll end up with a horse who's easy to catch and happy to see you.

Of course, our horses experience positive reinforcement every day without our thinking about it, and sometimes the results are not always what we're looking for. It can explain a lot of behavior that doesn't seem logical to us but makes perfect sense to the horse. "Hey," the horse thinks, "when my human walks in the barn in the morning, I paw the floor and yell, and *voilà!* Breakfast arrives. Works every time!" We may not think of this as positive reinforcement because we didn't intend to train the horse, but that's a classic example of a behavior that has developed through positive reinforcement.

Does positive reinforcement work? Yes, as long as the rewards are prompt and consistent. As with all training, if the rewards disappear, eventually the behavior will disappear.

Does positive reinforcement use bribes? No. There's a small but very important difference between a bribe and a reward. A bribe is given *before* the requested response; a reward *follows* the response. Remember, too, that the reward doesn't have to be food. There are other meaningful rewards the horse can appreciate, such as praise, rest, a scratch on the withers, or a rub on the forehead.

Negative Reinforcement

Negative reinforcement is *not* punishment. Negative reinforcement strengthens a particular behavior when the horse takes action to *avoid* something that's uncomfortable. When he responds correctly, he receives a clear reward because the negative condition *disappears.*

For example, to ask my horse to stop while I'm leading him, I stop walking and create pressure on the bridge of his nose by pulling back on the halter. The pressure is the negative condition: It's a small but uncomfortable pressure that upsets his balance and his comfort. The horse may attempt a couple of different responses to make the pressure go away, but it's only when he gives the correct response (he stops) that I promptly release the pressure. Through repetition, the horse learns that if he gives the correct response (stops), he receives a reward (the pressure goes away). *This is the important point*: The horse doesn't stop because I tug on the halter; he stops because he has learned that *every time* he responds in that way to that signal, the pressure goes away (or he avoids it entirely) and he is comfortable again. I'm not using physical force to stop a half-ton animal, I'm using a reward to encourage the horse to stop *by himself.*

To reinforce the correct behavior, I'll also give another reward, generally a pat or verbal praise—which is positive reinforcement.

If I use another signal a half-second before he feels the pressure on the noseband—if I stop walking and say "whoa" or raise my hand—the horse will begin to associate that secondary signal with the pressure on the noseband, and soon he'll halt when I simply say "whoa" and signal with body language. He's giving the correct response at the mere suggestion (or threat) of a negative condition. ("Aha," you say, "but if there's no negative condition to remove, what's the reward?") There are actually *two* rewards: He avoids the negative condition altogether, and he knows he's pleased me. More about the nature of rewards in chapter 3.)

Timing, of course, is critical. If I don't promptly reward the correct response—in other words, if I don't remove the pressure the moment my horse stops—then no learning takes place and he's likely to try a different response next time. If the horse receives a reward for *incorrect* behavior—if, for instance, he keeps walking and I let go of the halter—then I've taught him an incorrect and potentially dangerous behavior that will require stronger measures to correct.

So Which Works Better, Positive or Negative Reinforcement?

From the human point of view, training a horse through negative reinforcement (or a combination of negative and positive reinforcement) is often more effective than using positive reinforcement alone because negative reinforcement involves requests that are initiated by the trainer rather than the horse. Negative reinforcement prompts the horse to take action to relieve discomfort ("How do I get rid of that irritation?") instead of waiting for an otherwise comfortable, balanced, content horse to move toward a desired reward—which is essentially what has to happen with positive reinforcement.

It's important to remember that *every instance of negative or positive reinforcement must include the appropriate reward or it will not work.* The timing must *always* be precise, and the pattern must be *repeated* to strengthen the response because all training is based on logic, consistency, and repetition.

Punishment

Punishment (also called *correction*) teaches the horse that an incorrect behavior will result in an uncomfortable or undesirable consequence. He will therefore try to avoid the behavior, to avoid the consequences. With many horses, we do have to use punishment occasionally (and very carefully) to remind them that we, not they, are the team leaders. Older members of a herd would not tolerate a pushy, aggressive colt's obnoxious behavior, and we must not tolerate bad behavior, either—but the type and degree of punishment must always fit the transgression, and we need to remember that the *threat* of punishment often works better than actual punishment. And a horse must never, *ever* be punished for fearful or timid behavior or simply because the rider or trainer is impatient or angry.

Extinction

Extinction, the fourth pattern of learning, weakens a behavior by providing no feedback whatsoever. If a behavior never receives a reaction of any kind, positive or negative, it will gradually disappear. In training, this means two things. First, if the horse is no longer performing correctly, then we're probably developing a pattern of extinction by not providing any incentive for the correct behavior. We tend to focus on the requests we've made and the responses we get from our horses, but the critical factor from the horse's point of view is his reward. If you forget the reward, you're training by extinction, and that means you're *eliminating* desirable behavior. Second, if the horse persists in a behavior that we're trying to eliminate, then he must still be receiving some reward for it. It's easy to forget that the horse's rewards may come from the environment, the situation, or from animals or people other than ourselves.

Time and Memory

Some horses are able to remember the correct responses to things they haven't done for 10 years, while others seem to forget what they learned just last week. Studies have found that horses have excellent memories, so it's unlikely that a horse has forgotten what he learned. And it's not that one horse is smarter than another (although there are definite degrees of intelligence among horses). It's simply that the first horse was trained carefully and consistently, and his behavior patterns were reinforced so strongly that his response is nearly automatic, even years later. The horse who "forgets" never had his learning reinforced correctly or consistently, or some event has intervened to change the pattern of his behavior.

We've all heard riders moan, "Stupid horse! He did this just fine yesterday! Today I'm asking for the same thing the same way, and he's not doing it!" Meanwhile, the horse is thinking (if horses think as we do), "My response yesterday didn't work—there wasn't any reward—so I'll have to try something different today."

Combining the Learning Patterns

Successful communication with a horse is based largely on a combination of negative and positive reinforcement, plus occasional correction and extinction. All four patterns of learning are important, and you're likely to find yourself using two, three, or sometimes all four during one training exercise.

For instance, if you want to train your trail horse to walk quietly over a bridge, you might begin by placing a large sheet of plywood on the ground in his paddock. You put a carrot in the middle of the plywood and walk away. Eventually, the horse will become curious about the plywood or interested in the carrot or both, and he'll explore the plywood, sniff it, paw at it, and perhaps step on it to reach the food reward. You've left it entirely up to the horse to take his time and find the reward. He could see the carrot, but he couldn't reach it until he stepped on the obstacle. You gave him no commands, and there were no negative consequences if he didn't walk on the plywood. You've used straightforward, positive reinforcement to associate a reward with a specific behavior. And the horse is training himself—you don't even have to be there. You can be talking on the phone, cleaning stalls, or riding another horse.

Positive reinforcement can be very useful to introduce a horse to many strange and scary objects, and it should be part of every basic training program. But it's only part of the process because it doesn't teach him anything about trusting *you* and walking calmly across a bridge *at your request*. And some horses will be so fearful of any unfamiliar object that they'll simply stay far away from it, not wanting to step outside their comfort zone to risk their safety for something as trivial as a carrot.

But if your horse is willing to at least explore the plywood, next you move on to leading and then riding him across the plywood. If he balks or twists sideways, you might use a little negative reinforcement—a tap with a crop or a nudge with your heels—to create some discomfort, which he'll seek to avoid by looking for the correct response. Of course, you'll reinforce any attempt at the correct behavior with several rewards—the release of the irritation, a pat, and some verbal praise. After lots of practice to build his trust on the plywood, you'll ask him to transfer his learning and his trust in you to similar, but slightly more challenging, obstacles: a tarp, a raised dry bridge, a real bridge over a real stream in the woods.

Of course, before you ask your horse to walk over the plywood or anything else, you'll have spent many hours using negative *and* positive reinforcement to reward him for responding to a nudge from your legs or the verbal command "walk on." By the time you approach the bridge, he knows those signals *always* mean "walk forward," and he should also know he can trust you in scary situations. The best reward you can give your horse is to help him feel safe, secure, and confident in everything he does.

Would you use punishment or extinction in this training scenario? Almost never. If your horse is reluctant to walk over the bridge but doesn't seem truly fearful, you'll repeat the command to walk forward and be a little more forceful—after all, a good leader gives clear, *firm* directions. If your horse walks over the bridge willingly but acts a little worried and shows his concern by tossing his head or snorting, you'll reassure him and ignore the fussiness. The head tossing and snorting (signs of distress) should disappear if they are neither punished nor rewarded—that's extinction.

If, however, you give your horse a squeeze with your legs to ask him to step onto the plywood and he responds with dangerous, disrespectful behavior such as kicking or biting at your leg, then punishment may be appropriate. But if that happens, he clearly isn't ready to tackle obstacles—you first need to work on the basics of trust and respect.

For these geldings, dominance play is serious business—but they both understand that no one should be seriously injured. To establish a clear pecking order, horses use threats more than actual physical aggression. Whenever possible, trainers should make use of this, using threats rather than outright punishment to establish respect and obedience.

Trust, Respect, and Confidence

The training process is really about building trust and respect. When you have trust and respect, you'll have confidence. To develop these qualities in a horse, you need to introduce new tasks, situations, and problems in a logical, step-by-step program and show your horse that he can trust you to help him solve these problems. He can believe in you because you'll never, ever betray his trust or let him be hurt. You'll never ask him to do something he can't do or doesn't understand, and you'll never confuse him by changing the rules.

It's really easy to turn a steady, responsive, trustworthy horse into a resistant, anxious, ill-mannered one. People do it all the time through ignorance, inconsistency, misunderstanding, a need to dominate at all costs, or a simple lack of attention to the horse's needs. All you have to do is ignore the horse's good behavior (thereby extinguishing it), invite confrontation through indecision and confusion, ask for resistance by demanding more than the horse can give, send contradictory messages by rewarding him randomly, ignore his pain and insecurities, and punish him erratically to increase his anxiety.

The Horse's Hierarchy of Needs

Before anyone—human or horse—can focus on learning anything, certain basic needs must be met. In the 1950s, psychologist Abraham Maslow developed a theory of human psychology that is known as the Hierarchy of Needs and Self-Actualization. Maslow said that people must have their needs for air, food, water, and sex taken care of before they can seek the next level of needs—security and safety. Once all these lower-level needs are satisfied, people turn their attention to the next level of psychological needs, which includes love and esteem. If the lower levels are *not* met, a person cannot even think about anything on a higher level. For instance, abused children cannot learn to give or receive love until they feel safe; nor will they do well in school because learning can only take place at a higher level, which includes esteem. All their energy is taken up by trying to meet their more basic needs, and they can't concentrate on schoolwork until they are healthy, well-fed, safe, and secure.

Horses aren't as complex as we are—there's no evidence that they're striving for a human's highest desire for self-actualization, the "be all you can be" goal—but the basic hierarchy is remarkably similar. If your horse can't find enough food and water to survive, he's not going to be interested in your attempts to teach him flying changes. If a mare feels that she and her foal are being threatened by another horse, she will concentrate on that problem and ignore your requests to walk along quietly on the lead rope. And if all a stallion can think about is the band of mares in the next pasture, he'll do practically anything—ignoring his own safety and comfort—to satisfy that very primal need to reproduce.

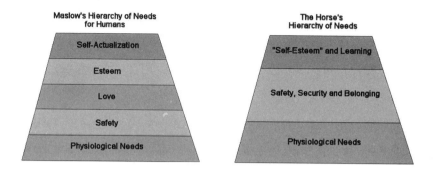

Although the horse's hierarchy of needs isn't as complex as ours, the same principles apply: The basic physiological needs for survival must be met before a horse can learn anything new.

So the physiological needs for sufficient food, water, shelter, and reproduction are primary, in horses as in humans. Next on the pyramid is the need to feel safe and secure. For the horse, this is met by familiar surroundings and the companionship of the herd. If there are no equine members in his herd—if he's an only horse—he'll turn to humans or to another species (such as a cat or a goat) for companionship. His barn represents security as well because it's familiar to him and that's where he finds food, water, and a safe place to sleep.

In the human hierarchy, Maslow separates safety and love/belonging into two separate levels, but for horses these two needs are very much intertwined. For the horse, the herd provides social order, which means a hierarchy, which represents safety. Being able to trust the herd and knowing where he fits into its social structure are absolutely critical to the horse's sense of security.

Familiar surroundings also represent safety and security. Familiar surroundings can mean different things for different horses; it all depends on what the horse has learned and experienced previously. (One of the basic goals in training is to expand the horse's concept of familiar surroundings so he will feel safe and be able to relax in many different situations.) A horse raised around llamas is comfortable with llamas; they represent familiar surroundings. But a mature horse who's suddenly confronted with llamas moving in next door will probably feel very threatened by these strange new creatures and will do his utmost to get away from the threat until time and experience prove to him that they're harmless.

Only after the needs for safety and security are met can learning take place. For humans, Maslow identifies learning as part of a need for esteem. When we humans learn new skills, we feel more confident in our ability to solve problems and manage new situations. For horses, learning is closely aligned with the need for security, which is also connected with obedience to the leader: The horse learns how to please the leader and he develops confidence in his ability to respond correctly so that he can feel safe and secure in his obedience.

Horses also seem to enjoy learning, especially when it involves physical activity. Becoming stronger, fitter, and better balanced often seems to increase a horse's self-confidence—and it may even improve his status in the herd, which certainly makes sense from a "survival of the fittest" perspective. The horse who can run faster, jump higher, and travel greater distances without fatigue is more likely to survive than his herdmates. Whether the horse can connect the human-directed learning activities with the positive physical results is uncertain, but there's no doubt that good physical activity releases feel-good endorphins in horses, just as it does in humans.

So why is this important? It's at the heart of understanding how horses learn. If your horse doesn't trust you—if he doesn't feel that his leader is going to keep him safe and secure—he's not going to be willing to learn how to step on that plywood bridge. No carrot will get him to walk into that trailer if he doesn't trust you.

2

WHAT HORSES REALLY
WANT US TO KNOW

So how can we figure out what our horses need and want?

The domesticated horse's agenda is established first by instinct and physical makeup and then by individual adaptations to his environment, which is largely controlled by humans. The horse's instinctive behaviors are solidly based on three biological characteristics: his superb physical adaptations that give him the power to run first and ask questions later, his place in the food chain as a prey animal, and his position within the social dynamics of the herd. These three characteristics are the foundation of millions of years of evolutionary success.

Physiological Needs

The horse's instincts tell him that he must *always* be able to do the following four things.

Move Freely

The ability to flee from danger (real or imagined) is essential. The horse who ignores movement in the undergrowth might become someone's lunch. Many things can threaten a horse's security about his ability to run away. A horse's instincts tell him that having his feet stuck in mud or tangled in vines, walking on a slippery or unsteady surface, or stepping into a puddle that just might turn out to be a bottomless pit are all potentially life-threatening situations.

Movement is also necessary to help the horse's body function properly. We've all seen horses who "stock up" when they're stallbound: Lymphatic fluid collects in their lower legs, and they stiffen up when they can't move around freely. Walking and running keeps horses more comfortable because the movement of the feet acts as a secondary circulation pump to push blood and lymph back up the legs toward the heart. When movement is restricted, blood and lymphatic fluid tend to pool in the lower legs, and those feet can become sore, especially in cold weather. A horse who kicks the walls of his stall may simply being trying to say that his feet hurt and he needs to move around more.

The horse's digestion works better, too, when he can move freely. All that vegetable matter needs to travel a very long distance through the horse's gut, and regular exercise helps move it along.

What this means in training:

- Allowing your horse to move forward freely can be a reward for him. Release from restrictions can also be a reward.

- To keep your horse from panicking when he can't run away from danger, you'll need to develop his trust.

- Keeping a horse stallbound can make him physically uncomfortable and promote boredom, which can encourage stable vices.

- Much of what we ask a horse to do goes against his nature, so careful training is necessary to develop a horse's trust in humans and overcome his instinctive need to startle and flee from new sights and sounds and to panic in confining situations.

Eat Frequently

The horse is a grass-eating, open-plains animal, and that means his digestive system is most comfortable when he can eat small amounts of low-protein, high-fiber grass, preferably while moving from place to place with the herd. Horses on pasture commonly spend three-quarters of their waking hours grazing. A grazing horse can be easily startled away from food if danger approaches.

What this means in training:

- Horses are accustomed to having food spread out over a large area, where no one has to compete or be crowded into a small space to eat.

- Safety is higher on the horse's priority list than food, so a fearful horse will not respond to a food reward.

- A horse doesn't consider food to be a reward in the same way a dog does. For the pastured horse, food is something that's pretty much there all the time, underfoot. It's not a prize that has to be hunted down and killed or acquired through vigorous activity.

Seek Physical Comfort and Avoid Physical Discomfort

Physical comfort includes the reassurance of touch, which reminds horses that they're not alone and makes them feel good by stimulating the release of endorphins. Physical comfort also includes feelings of health, well-being, confidence, and strength and balance in movement.

Discomfort includes all the obvious conditions, such as pain, cold, sickness, and hunger, but it can also take less-obvious forms, such as a loss of equilibrium, pressure against a sensitive spot, or the too-close presence of a more dominant animal.

What this means in training:

- Touch can be either a reward or a source of discomfort.

- The trainer must know how, when, where, and how much physical pressure to apply or release to ask the horse to change his balance, position, or motion.

- A horse who is sick or in pain cannot focus on the subtler forms of physical touch used in training.

Keep the Gene Pool Alive

This is an imperative for both for mares and stallions. When hormones kick in during a mare's estrous (fertile) cycle, or a mare has a foal who needs protecting, her priorities can change—sometimes rather drastically. Hormonal changes can cause a nondominant mare to become combative, a dominant mare to become passive, or a normally well-behaved stallion to become downright single-minded (and possibly dangerous) in the presence of a mare in estrous.

What this means in training:

- Most stallions are preprogrammed to challenge the leader and defend the herd. To manage a stallion and maintain your leadership position, you must always be vigilant and ready to back up your requests with logic, firmness, and prompt threats or corrections when necessary. And you must never get into a physical battle that you can't win!

- If you work with a mare or a stallion, you must gain a thorough understanding of how hormonal changes and instincts can affect that particular horse. Tailor your management and training techniques to accommodate or circumvent those changes. Be firm and stay flexible.

Safety and Security Needs

Your horse believes with every fiber of his being that these four behaviors will keep him safe and secure.

Stay with the Herd

Horses are very social creatures. The herd is the source of safety, friendship, and education. The strong horses protect the weaker ones, the older horses teach the younger ones, and it's always good to have a grooming buddy who will scratch the itchy spots and help chase away flies. Fortunately for us, horses are willing to include humans as part of the herd.

From the horse's point of view, the herd is the source of safety, friendship, and education. Fortunately, most horses are willing to accept humans as members of the herd, but it's up to us to determine how we will function within the herd—either as effective leaders or as passive followers. There is no equality in a herd.

What this means in training:

- If you are part of his herd, your horse will offer his trust to you. It's yours to keep or lose.
- Companionship is a powerful reward, and your horse may consider solitary confinement as a severe form of punishment.
- You can simulate grooming-buddy rubs and pats to reassure and reward your horse.

Obey the Leader

Every horse needs to understand his place in the group. Leaders become leaders because they are strong, confident, and consistent in explaining the rules. Leaders know how to find food, water, and shelter, and how to avoid danger. Every foal learns to follow leaders, first by following his dam and then by watching all the other older, wiser horses.

What this means in training:

- When a horse accepts you as his wise, confident, trustworthy leader, he'll happily follow your directions because he knows you'll keep him safe and take care of his physical needs.

- Your training must always be clear, consistent, and logical, or your horse may elect a new leader.

- You can make good use of a steady, experienced horse to help train younger ones.

- A steady, confident leader helps create steady, confident herd members. But a nervous, fearful leader generates nervousness and fear in the rest of the herd.

If the Leader Fails to Lead, Someone Else Must Step In

Someone has got to be in charge, make the decisions, and enforce the rules—or danger can sneak in. If there's a leadership vacuum, most horses are willing to step into the role, especially if the other herd members (equine or human) show weakness, inconsistency, or a lack of confidence.

What this means in training:

- You mustn't allow a leadership vacuum to develop.

- But sometimes you'll need to trust your horse and temporarily give him the leadership role.

Respond to a Threat *before* You Get Hurt

One horse usually dominates another by using threatening gestures, not by inflicting pain. Horses need to respect and obey the herd leaders to stay safe from external dangers, but the herd wouldn't last long if the dominant horses inflicted frequent, serious injuries on the lesser members of the herd. Leaders make their demands known by pushing, bumping, charging, pinning their ears, baring their teeth, squealing, and *threatening* to kick or bite. It's only when these forms of communication don't get the message across, or when the target of the threat can't get out of the way quickly enough, that the threats escalate to actual violence.

What this means in training:

- A horse is intimidated by someone who acts with supreme confidence and moves abruptly. If you can outmaneuver a pushy, domineering horse, he's going to believe that you are faster and stronger than he is, and you could have done him serious harm—but chose not to. The flip side of this is that a nervous, sensitive, already submissive horse will be made even more fearful by quick, powerful movements, so you must always be able to tailor your behavior to the needs of the situation and the individual horse.

- As training progresses, the trainer's requests can (and should) become more and more subtle, and the horse's responses should become more and more prompt and sensitive.

Self-Esteem and Learning Needs

After their basic physical and security needs are met, horses can turn their attention to these three behaviors.

Satisfy Your Curiosity

Nearly all horses display a strong sense of curiosity when they don't feel threatened. By satisfying his curiosity, a horse learns whom he can trust and what items or situations he can ignore. If *everything* is seen as a threat—if the horse remains on constant high alert and he never learns to trust anything—there's no energy left for him to respond to real danger or to learn.

What this means in training:

- Curiosity is a powerful tool in training because the horse's desire to know can overcome mild anxiety about new surroundings and unfamiliar challenges. Curiosity usually exists just outside a horse's comfort zone: If something is different enough to spark attention and curiosity and is safely presented and not so threatening that it creates fear, the horse will initiate learning on his own.

- Curiosity can also get your horse into trouble. Many interesting items are dangerous as horse toys, such as an empty glass jug, a rusty piece of farm equipment lying in a pasture, or exposed electrical wiring.

Learn through Play

Horses, like all mammals, use play behaviors to explore their environment, learn new skills, and establish relationships with one another.

What this means in training:

- If we think of training as constructive play, not just disciplined task learning, we can change our relationships with our horses from master and servant to coach and team member—and both the horse and the human can take turns being the coach.

- A horse needs time to play (experiment) with some of the new skills he's learning. Making room for play in many areas of learning (think of cutting cattle, jumping, crossing a stream, lead changes) can help create a happy, willing partner instead of merely a dull, obedient one.

Give your horse a chance to play safely as he explores his environment and learns new skills.

The Wise Young Gelding

Two horses who were pastured together at our stable, an old mare named Eva and a younger gelding named Storm, enjoyed each other's companionship and maintained a harmonious relationship for several years. They grazed side by side and munched from separate but equal piles of hay placed far apart. To feed them their grain, I attached buckets to two outside walls under the roof overhang of their run-in shed: Storm's bucket on a side wall and Eva's bucket around the corner on the back wall, so they were well separated while they ate their grain.

I always fed Eva first, which gave her a little extra time to eat; she was a slow eater, and she needed more feed because of her age. The arrangement worked well because although Storm, an easy keeper, always finished first, Eva was dominant. She was easily able to keep him away from her feed bucket with an occasional threat reminder: flattened ears, shaking head, and a hind foot raised in warning if he so much as approached her side of the barn. Eva never had to follow through on her threats because Storm's mother had raised him right and taught him to have a healthy respect for cranky old ladies. After he finished his grain, Storm generally stood a safe distance back and simply watched longingly as Eva slowly vacuumed up every last kernel from her feed tub.

The balance of power at dinnertime shifted unexpectedly, however, after Storm went into training for trail classes. For several days, I concentrated on sharpening his ability to step slowly and precisely backward through various barriers, poles on the ground, and tarps draped between jump standards, all set up as zigzags or L-shaped grids. Storm caught on quickly and seemed to enjoy learning how to move slowly and deliberately backward through the obstacles, executing small turns on his forehand or haunches wherever necessary. Food had always been a real motivator for

Get Stronger and You May Move Up in the Hierarchy

The hierarchy of a herd is a fluid thing, and horses are constantly challenging one another for the chance to move up.

What this means in training:

- Horses who develop strength, stamina, experience, physical agility, and new skills through human-directed training programs may also gain more status in the equine herd (although your horse probably won't understand that he has you to thank for this!).

- Strong, knowledgeable horses may challenge their riders more often. Timid or inexperienced riders often have trouble gaining the respect and trust of confident, experienced, physically fit horses, who may remain convinced that they know more than their riders.

Storm, so I sometimes rewarded his good performance with a carrot during a training break.

One morning at breakfast, a few days after Storm had begun his trail class training, I was surprised to see the gelding eating happily from Eva's feed tub while she stood uncertainly near his already-empty bucket. Neither horse bore any battle scars, but some drastic restructuring of their relationship had obviously occurred.

At dinner that night, I fed them according to the usual pattern—first the mare and then the gelding—and sat down nearby to watch. After Storm finished his grain at the side of the shed, he carefully turned so his body was parallel to the shed wall and he was facing toward the front, away from the back where Eva was still eating. Then, stepping precisely *backward*, he moved very slowly along the wall, executed a perfect 90-degree turn at the corner of the shed and continued to step backward along the back wall until he was next to Eva's feed tub. He never issued a direct challenge, kicked, or threatened her in any way but instead used his rather large rump to gently push Eva away from her bucket and earn his own food reward for good performance.

Once he had his head in her feed tub, he simply performed a few quarter-turns on the forehand and used his hindquarters to keep her away. The mare, who was accustomed to handling head-on confrontations, couldn't figure out how to respond to Storm's indirect approach, and so she simply gave ground, flicking her ears and swishing her tail in what I could only assume was confusion and frustration.

The only way to preserve Eva's mental health and physical condition—and make sure she got her correct share of the food—was to close Storm inside the run-in shed during meals.

Gender Influences

Mares are born to be mothers, and mothers must be bosses. They must take on the responsibility of teaching the next generation how to survive and behave in the herd, and most mares understand this job quite well.

The lead (alpha) mare in a herd decides where and when to find food, water, and shelter; where to rest safely at night; how and when a youngster will be disciplined; and what position a new horse will occupy in the herd's social order. In a large band, two or more alpha mares may share these duties. Dominant mares tend to raise dominant foals because the foals learn from their moms how to relate to other members of the herd—and, by extension, how to relate to humans. Studies of orphan foals show that biological daughters of alpha mares, when adopted by nondominant mares, will usually end up lower in the herd's hierarchy than their biological dams had been.

This tendency of mares to be in charge can be both a blessing and a curse. Many trainers will insist that mares learn more quickly and are more capable of thinking for themselves than stallions or geldings; other trainers refuse to work with mares because of their difficult personalities. Mares vary widely in their response to hormonal swings, as well. Some will remain steady and consistent in their behavior no matter what the time of month or year, while others will become grumpy, stubborn, or downright mean during their receptive periods.

It can be difficult to convince an alpha mare that a human is in charge because the human's wishes may not be at the top of her agenda. She may just be too busy protecting a foal, staying alert for danger, focusing on reproductive needs, or maintaining the social order within her group.

The stallion's role is chief protector of the harem. His main role in a wild band is to collect mares and defend his band from external threats so that he can pass on his DNA to as many foals as possible. Unless it's breeding season or he has to chase off something that may harm or steal his mares, he's often perfectly happy having the mares tell him what to do and where to go. If there are no mares around to fuss over, stallions can live and work quite happily beside other stallions. They can also become loyal, hardworking partners for people who understand them and know how to manage their instincts and macho behavior. However, stallions must be handled only by people who can establish a strong leadership position and reinforce the horse's respect whenever necessary because when a stallion challenges his human partner for dominance, serious injury can result.

Geldings are the darlings of horse-human partnerships. They have all the same needs for companionship and security as other horses, but they don't have to listen to hormones, defend a harem, or be anybody's parent. Although there may be an alpha gelding in any mixed group, he will often defer to the boss mare when she's present. Geldings are generally accustomed to taking orders from someone else, so they can usually transfer their loyalty and obedience quite easily from equine to human herd members.

The Herd's Social Hierarchy

Human relationships are based on equality. We tell our children that true friends don't try to dominate or manipulate one another. But relationships among horses are never equal. Instead, they're based on a pecking order, a social hierarchy that is critical to the smooth functioning of the herd. The hierarchy will shift from time to time as individuals age, mares go through their hormonal cycles, and new herd members come and go, but the pecking order will generally remain fairly stable in any unchanging group of horses. The top-ranking horse will be first to eat, first to walk through the gate, and first at the water trough. The lowest-ranking member of the herd must hang back and wait for every one else to drink and eat or risk receiving a nip or kick.

To us, this sounds unfair. From the horse's point of view, however, this arrangement provides security and safety. To remain safe and secure, each horse must know where he stands in the herd's hierarchy. When an outside threat looms, the weakest member of the herd will be protected by the strongest, and the youngest is guided by the most experienced. For this to work, each horse has to know who is weakest and who is strongest.

Don't try to change a horse's low status in the herd—it won't work. If you walk into a herd of loose horses and offer food to a horse who's low in the pecking order, you're inviting jealousy, turmoil, and possible injury. If you try to lead the low-ranking horse through the gate first while the alpha horse is standing beside the gate, the horse you're leading will be reluctant or even frightened to go through the gate. The dominant horse assumes it's his job to get through the gate first, and if you're forcing the lower-order horse to challenge that, someone may get hurt. And the horses will have to reestablish the pecking order again later because you've temporarily upset the group's hierarchy. They will remain at peace only as long as everyone clearly understands their position in the herd.

So how can you give your nondominant horse extra food or get safely through the gate? Remove him from the herd and *then* feed him. Ask someone with authority to hold the other horse or tie the bossy one out of the way temporarily while you lead your horse through the gate. Don't ask your horse to do something that he *knows* is going to get him punished by the alpha horse!

When a new horse enters the group, there will be a good deal of scuffling and challenging, possibly biting and kicking, until everyone knows where the new horse fits into the herd. To minimize turmoil and potential injury, introduce a new horse to an easy-going, middle-of-the-pack member, let them become buddies over a stall wall or in adjacent paddocks, and then ease both of them into the herd. With this more gradual method, the horses get acquainted in safer circumstances, and the eventual hierarchy battles will probably be more symbolic than dangerous.

When you are riding or working your horse in a group, herd-hierarchy issues will arise and must be firmly dealt with. For safety's sake, each human must remain *above* her horse in the hierarchy. You must insist on good manners, asking your horses to put aside their herd issues and work quietly next to other horses—regardless of their relationship preferences.

Personality Types

Horses are all different, of course, but we can look at individual horses, identify certain personality types, and then use that knowledge to tailor our training to our horses.

Friendly or Standoffish

Some horses are gregarious and very friendly toward other horses and humans. Horses raised in a large, boisterous group are like children in a large family— they're most comfortable with lots of activity and plenty of friends always

Emily Singer

High-performance horses need an extra measure of dominance and energy to be successful. The characteristics that create success in competition—boldness, sensitivity, and reactivity—usually make these horses unsuitable for beginners or timid riders.

around, and they probably have a good grasp of the social dynamics of the herd. Being with their friends is extremely important to them, and they are accustomed to learning from others and finding their place in the hierarchy.

Other horses, particularly those who have spent lots of time in large training barns or at racetracks (where they can see other horses but can't develop true herd relationships), may be more aloof. The close proximity of other horses may make them nervous because they haven't had a chance to make friends in a natural group setting and they don't understand herd dynamics. They may be less willing to take orders from (or trust) another horse or a human because they've had to rely more on themselves to stay safe and secure.

A friendly horse is often a curious horse. He'll be the first to greet a new person or investigate a new piece of equipment. A standoffish horse, on the other hand, is more comfortable standing back and considering new herd members from a distance. Some horses who demonstrate aloofness may also be more fearful in new situations. Their self-protection instincts are stronger than their instincts to investigate and follow. Other aloof horses aren't fearful, just a little slow to form attachments.

Energetic or Phlegmatic

Energy level is often a breed characteristic—hence the terms hot-, cold-, and warmblooded. A hotblooded, high-energy horse will put extra effort into everything—eating, playing, running, climbing hills, jumping, greeting his friends, and displaying his likes and dislikes. He has a terrific work ethic and usually tackles new tasks willingly, but he can be exhausting for a rider who just wants to mosey along on the trails.

The overly relaxed, phlegmatic horse conserves his energy and has to be urged into physical activity. He has a nice calming influence on the young horses, and he can be the darling of the lesson barn, but he's also frustratingly dull for the experienced rider.

Curious or Fearful

All horses harbor fears—it's the nature of a prey animal. Recognizing threats and responding promptly with flight or fight (preferably flight) has kept the horse alive for millions of years. But each horse varies in his level of instinctive fearfulness, and some horses seem to retain a high level of fear and mistrust despite careful handling and training. A tendency to startle and spook does run in certain family lines, especially in the hotblooded breeds, which makes sense. After all, for thousands of years, humans have bred Thoroughbreds and Arabians for speed, agility, sensitivity, fire, and brilliance, which are all simply manifestations of a horse's ability to run first and ask questions later.

A horse's fear is overcome or balanced by curiosity and, of course, trust in his companions. A horse with lots of fear but no curiosity or trust is dangerous because his fears will overwhelm him and create panic, and panic leads to injury, which, of course, simply confirms the horse's original fear of being hurt.

Dominant or Submissive

In his book *Resistance-Free Training,* Richard Shrake uses a military analogy to categorize horses as generals, captains, or privates. The generals are in charge, the captains take orders from the generals but also command the lower troops, and the privates get pushed around by everyone. Shrake notes that although the generals often become the top performance horses, they're also the ones who will challenge you every step of the way, so they take longer to train. The privates are also frustrating to train because they tend to be timid and lacking in self-confidence. Every horse needs a certain amount of the dominance characteristic to also have confidence in himself.

It's the captains who respond best to human demands because they most easily accept humans as their leaders, but they will also think for themselves and retain the training they receive.

What's the "Best" Personality?

It depends, of course, on what sort of horse you prefer. A cutting horse or open jumper needs to have more than an average dose of dominance, fearlessness, and energy to be truly successful. A child's pleasure horse should be fearless, too, but also friendly and a little slow.

Some personality combinations are volatile. As I've already mentioned, a fearful, energetic, unfriendly, and overly submissive horse is extremely difficult to work with because that type of horse may never learn to fully trust humans or other horses. A high-energy, dominant, fearless horse can be dangerous because it's nearly impossible to gain his respect. And a lethargic, dull, aloof horse with little curiosity in his surroundings can't be fully trusted to learn and make wise decisions to keep himself and others safe.

Fortunately, most horses fall somewhere in the middle ranks for all personality traits. They are friendly but also willing to leave the herd. They are energetic enough to get the job done but also willing to pause and relax. They are not aggressively dominant but are willing to take the lead when necessary. They are cautious but curious and trusting, so they can safely investigate new situations. These are the horses who will respond to our requests and let us know how they feel about the horse-human relationship, if we simply pay attention.

3

PORTRAIT OF THE TRAINER AS A WISE OLD MARE

Good training promotes trust and obedience, but it also develops the horse's judgment and sense of responsibility. We want our horse to trust us, but we need to be able to trust the horse, too. We want the horse to be responsible for his actions—to understand causes and consequences and to choose actions that will keep us both safe and comfortable.

Am I anthropomorphizing? I don't think so. We can't force horses into reliable obedience, and we can't force them to trust us. Horses have to choose to do what we want them to do.

Some trainers try to insist on blind obedience. They don't want the horse to think for himself. It's a tribute to a horse's kind and willing temperament when a trainer manages to achieve this level of submission. But if I'm in full gallop on a trappy cross-country course, I don't have *time* to tell my horse how to meet every jump. When we cross a river, it's my horse who needs to feel for the safe passage—I can't tell him where to put his feet. I want a horse who tackles these problems with confidence and skill, not one who's tentative and uncertain, waiting for me to micromanage every movement.

How to Be a Wise Old Mare

The alpha mare makes group decisions for the herd by controlling the horses' movements and their access to resources. She has to make the right decisions, or the herd's safety will suffer and her authority will be challenged by others who think they know better.

How did the wise old mare become wise and dominant? Through experience, learning, and the ability to make decisions and project confidence. These are essential components of leadership.

Horses learn from their own experiences, of course, but they also learn by observing others. Watch a group of horses moving into a new pasture and you'll

31

see a variety of approaches and responses to the new environment. The older, more experienced horses are likely to amble in and casually explore their space, demonstrating exactly how best to investigate a new environment: with calmness, confidence, and a balance of curiosity and caution that will keep them safe while they learn about their surroundings. They might be saying, "Interesting, yes, good grass over here. Where's the water? Okay, let's look for gopher holes. Hey, look, there's a large rock. Let's check it out."

Younger and less experienced horses will snort and leap and lurch and bounce off one another in a frantic effort to sort out the dangerous from the nondangerous. You can almost hear these horses saying to one another, *"What's safe? Where do I go?* Nothing looks right! *You* go first!" or "Eek! Okay, that's a rabbit, not dangerous. Over there, though, it smells like wolves—stay alert!"

The learning process is all about expanding the knowledge base, having new experiences, and then making judgments based on what happens next: comfort or discomfort, rewards or no rewards, safety or danger. This applies to all new experiences, not just physical surroundings. A horse who hasn't yet learned to balance himself and his rider in a steady lope will not be comfortable if you try to teach him flying changes. If you push for too much too soon, his response may very well be similar to the young horse turned loose in the new pasture: "I don't feel safe. What do you want me to do? I feel clumsy, and I don't understand how to do this, and someone's going to get hurt!"

You are your domesticated horse's leader, so you have to be the wise old mare. You have to develop your horse's trust and confidence in your wise decisions as you guide him through experiences that will teach *him* how to discriminate and make good choices. You're going to develop his knowledge base and tell him what the best behavior is so that even in new situations he will remain calm, obey the leader, and also think for himself.

The Twelve Principles of Positive Horse Training

Since we humans intend to be the herd leaders for our horses, we have certain responsibilities. These responsibilities form the underlying principles of positive horse training.

Never Punish Fear

Our horses have to do many things they don't really want to do: have their feet trimmed and shod, stand still for inoculations and fly spray, walk away from their friends, step into trailers, and walk over bridges. Our responsibilities—to our farriers and veterinarians, as well as to our horses—include teaching every horse not to be afraid of these things.

Fear is *not* a challenge to your authority. If you punish a horse for being afraid, he'll simply become more confirmed in his fear because he'll associate pain and punishment with the scary object or situation. Your job when your horse is frightened is to increase his comfort and safety and decrease his fear—not the opposite. If you want to have a calm, confident, courageous horse, you must be the calm, confident, courageous leader.

It's easy to recognize the difference between fear and willful disobedience. When a horse is afraid, his breathing and heart rate will increase. His ears and eyes will focus intently on the frightening object, and he will try to simultaneously escape and keep it in view. He may roll his eyes, become agitated, break out in a sweat, or—in really severe cases of anxiety—show symptoms of colic. (See chapter 14 for how to systematically deprogram the fear response.)

Say Thank You

Rewarding frequently, promptly, and appropriately is the way you thank your horse. Every time you reward your horse, you're saying yes by giving him positive feedback that reinforces the correct response. And whenever your horse says yes to your requests, remember to say thank you with a reward.

Reward according to the request and the response. If you're asking your horse to do something big—something very difficult or completely new—your reward should also be big.

Be sure to reward *any* attempt on the part of your horse to understand and give the correct response, especially if you're introducing something new. Learning is a step-by-step process, not a sudden revelation. Reward every attempt, every little sign of progress, not just the complete performance. (As Richard Shrake says, "Reward the try.")

And reward immediately! If, for instance, you ask your horse to perform a turn, a flying change, and a halt, there must be three rewards for the three requests, and each reward must promptly follow the specific behavior. For the horse who has performed all three of these maneuvers before, the rewards might be fairly subtle—a quieting of the aids after the turn, a lightening of the leg and seat after the change, and then a pat and praise and full relaxation after the halt—but each demand-response cycle *must* be followed by an appropriate reward. For the horse who is just beginning to learn flying changes, the appropriate reward for that one movement would be very large, very clear, and not followed immediately by *any* other demands.

Say Please

Horses hate surprises, so preparation for a command counts. Give your horse a small signal that something is about to change or a request is about to be made, *before* you ask for the response. Your please can be anything from a straightening of your shoulders or a turn of your head to a full-blown half-halt, depending on what's about to follow.

Use Good Stress, Not Distress

Your horse has not signed on for the "no pain, no gain" program. Drilling him until he turns sour and resistant should *never* be part of the training process. Remember, however, that for any learning (mental or physical) to take place, there must be work—that's good stress. Muscles need to be pushed just a little further, the brain has to be engaged with new problems, and the edges of the horse's comfort zone need to be stretched.

We think of physical overexertion as the main source of distress for horses, but there are many other sources of bad stress. Psychological causes of distress can include solitary confinement or limited interaction with other horses, forced interaction among horses who dislike or distrust one another, stabling in a competitive environment, or anything that causes fear and uncertainty. Manage all aspects of your horse's care so that he remains healthy and comfortable.

Leave Your Personal Baggage at Home

Horses live in the present, but they have long memories. Your horse will not understand that you had a fight with your boyfriend or didn't get that promotion, so if you carry your personal anger into the riding arena, you're setting yourself up for frustration, defeat, and possible injury.

Apply corrections quickly, clearly, and logically. You *must* promptly correct disrespectful behavior and bad manners, but you can't expect your horse to trust and respect you if you suddenly become angry, hurtful, and unpredictable. If you can't manage your emotions when you're working with your horse, go to the gym or pound a pillow or talk to a friend.

On the plus side, horses are remarkably forgiving when you make an honest mistake. They don't plot revenge or scheme to get you back later, and they don't hold personal grudges.

Understand That Your Natural Aids Are Your Most Important Communication Tools

Fancy gear and expensive gadgets can't make up for poor basics. Your natural aids—hands, legs, voice, and weight (balance)—are the most important tools you have for communicating with your horse. Many people devote many hours and many dollars in a quest for the perfect saddle or exactly the right bit that will magically give them a fluid sitting trot or smooth flying changes or a great sliding stop, when the solution is really just a matter of balance and focus and hard work. You can always improve on what you were born with; a good trainer never stops learning!

Encourage Your Horse's Curiosity and Sense of Play

Curious is the opposite of fearful, and playful is the opposite of dull and boring. All mammals learn life skills through play. Just be sure playtime is safe for both of you. Swimming with your horse can be fun when you're both prepared for it, but if he lies down to roll in an icy stream in winter, that can be deadly. Running and bucking in his paddock is a good way for him to get rid of excess energy, but bucking when you're riding him is dangerous. Most horses thoroughly enjoy trail rides and jumping, which can serve as welcome breaks in heavy training schedules.

Keep the Lines of Communication Clear

As noted dressage instructor Lendon Gray says, "Don't clutter up the lines with chatter." If your legs are constantly bumping, nagging, swinging, poking, and nudging against your horse's sides, what are you asking him to do? If your hands are always fidgeting, adjusting, and flipping the reins, how is the horse supposed to respond? Is he supposed to ignore all that background static and then be able to pick out the one nudge or tug or weight shift that he should respond to? Develop the habit of riding every horse very quietly. Keep your legs against your horse's side in a clingy, wet-towel way until you're ready to use them. Then make your requests very clear, separate, and uncluttered—there should be a moment of nothing before the request and a moment of nothing after it.

Ask, then *listen* to the response! In a human conversation, are you constantly thinking about the next witty thing you're going to say instead of listening to the other person? Trainers and riders often do the same thing to horses. They are so self-absorbed and goal directed that they never hear the response from the horse—they simply push on to the next movement, the next demand, or the next item on *their* list. Keep the lines of communication clear and *open*.

Plan Your Ride and Ride Your Plan

Resistance is never personal; it's a response to something that's wrong. Therefore, resistance is simply a problem to be solved. Good trainers are able to set goals, create a road map so that they know where they want to go, understand the step-by-step training and learning processes, identify problems, make detours as needed, and recognize success.

Good trainers also need the flexibility to recognize when to change their expectations and set the road map aside. Horse training is art as well as science, and things very often do not proceed according to plan. So if something's not working, make a new plan. You must also be able to understand your limitations, identify those horses you cannot succeed with, recognize the situations you cannot manage, and gracefully step aside. When in doubt, get help!

Keep Your Horse and Yourself Safe from *True* Danger

Try to eliminate dangers you cannot control. Clutter in the barn aisles, broken fencing, farm equipment left in the pasture, wheelbarrows parked with handles protruding, exposed electrical wiring, baling twine, and hay nets left dangling where a foot can get caught—these are all dangerous, panic-creating traps that you *don't* want your horse to have to deal with, with or without your help and guidance. (However, as a conscientious trainer, you'll also teach your horse how to accept entrapments and other situations that might trigger a panic response.)

Your natural aids are the most important communication tools you have. Always work to improve your balance, control, and precise use of the aids.

Create *Simulated* Danger That You Can Control

Give your horse the tools to deal with scary stuff. At some point, your horse will probably have to walk through a too-narrow doorway, stand next to a noisy school bus, or step through a tangle of leg-entrapping tree limbs. You can't wrap him in cotton padding, and you can't avoid or control all unexpected dangers. Therefore, you *must* help him learn to handle his fears in carefully controlled settings so that he will develop his ability to remain calm in the face of threats and potential disasters. Often called *bombproofing* or *combat training,* this very important training introduces the horse to a wide variety of fear-inducing situations in a safe, trust-building way. (See chapter 14 for combat training exercises.)

Understand Your Horse's Comfort Zones

Learning generally happens in small increments, not huge leaps, and it happens when we push just a *little* bit outside the horse's repertoire of known challenges and solutions. If the challenge demands too big a step outside the comfort zone,

---

The Twelve Principles of Positive Horse Training

1. Never punish fear.
2. Say thank you by rewarding your horse frequently, promptly, and appropriately.
3. Say please by preparing your horse for a command.
4. Use good stress, not distress.
5. Apply corrections quickly, clearly, and logically, and leave your personal baggage at home.
6. Understand that your natural aids—hands, legs, voice, and weight (balance)—are the most important tools you have for communicating with your horse.
7. Encourage your horse's curiosity and sense of play.
8. Keep the lines of communication open and clear.
9. Plan your ride and ride your plan; if something's not working, make a new plan.
10. Keep your horse safe from *true* danger.
11. Create *simulated* danger that you can control.
12. Understand your horse's comfort zones and learning zones, and don't demand more than he can give.

---

all you'll get is resistance, anxiety, and an "I can't!" response. In his "pizza" approach to training, trainer Richard Shrake stresses the need to break the learning tasks into manageable bites. Don't ask your horse to swallow the whole thing at once!

The Seven Key Concepts of Positive Horse Training

Positive training relies on understanding seven key concepts, all of which are critical to developing a horse's trust, confidence, and willing obedience.

The Comfort Zone

Your horse's comfort zone is where he feels knowledgeable, experienced, and confident. When he's in his comfort zone, he moves forward willingly or stands quietly and responds with no signs of anxiety or reluctance.

A newborn foal's comfort zone is no larger than his mother's shadow—that's the *only* place he feels safe and secure because that's where food and shelter and protection and knowledge all reside. With his mother's encouragement and good example, the foal gradually expands his knowledge of the world by venturing outside that first tiny comfort zone, pushing the boundaries outward a little more each day. Then other horses and humans can step in, to provide role models and help build trust and confidence.

The Learning Zone

The greatest learning takes place just outside a comfort zone, where the horse will be challenged but not overly so. Like the comfort zone, the learning zone varies for each horse and each situation.

Your green jumper's comfort zone may include a two-foot crossrail but not a three-foot coop. You can't just charge at the coop and hope he'll figure it out. To get him to approach and comfortably jump the coop, you need to move from his comfort zone into his learning zone. Push him just a little more each time—perhaps by introducing him to two-foot vertical jumps, then to a two-and-a-half-foot vertical made from wide planks. Soon his learning zone and eventually his comfort zone will expand to include the coop because he can build on his earlier knowledge to solve the new problem. For each horse and each situation, you need to know where the comfort zone is and how far outside it you can move because that's where learning takes place.

The Reward Cycle

The reward cycle for basic learning consists of three parts: The trainer makes a request, the horse responds, and the trainer rewards the correct response. Be sure to allow time for the horse to consider possible responses, and expect to have to repeat the request if you don't get the correct response. If you ignore the incorrect responses and if you give prompt, consistent, appropriate rewards for the correct response, your horse should quickly connect the request to the response and reward and soon begin anticipating the pleasant consequences of his efforts.

Remember, you're not simply training for specific behaviors. Rather, you're teaching your horse trust, respect, obedience, confidence, and a pattern for future learning.

The reward cycle for changing bad behavior to good behavior may require an extra step, so the cycle may have to be as follows: request, wrong response, correction, request, right response, reward. If you're using a strong correction or punishment to extinguish dangerous behavior, you may have to repeat the cycle several times to clearly explain what you're looking for—but you must also give a big reward when the response is correct.

The Rewards Toolbox

This is your collection of rewards tools, which will vary from one training situation to the next. Regardless of where you are and what the task is, you'll want to have as many tools in your rewards toolbox as possible, and your tools should always include both primary and secondary rewards. (See page 40 for a discussion of the nature of rewards.)

Combat Training

Sometimes called bombproofing or spookproofing, this low-threat, confidence-building program introduces scary objects and simulated dangers that push the edge of your horse's comfort zone and help him learn that you *can* be trusted and you *must* be respected because *you* hold the keys to his safety, comfort, and peace of mind.

Trust Builders

Every experience is a trust builder if it reinforces your horse's trust, confidence, and respect for you—his leader.

Trust Busters

Any time your horse gets hurt, sore, or badly frightened as a result of your poor leadership decisions, that's a major trust buster. Other trust busters include situations in which you fail to lead, fail to reward good behavior, or fail to command respect.

The Seven Key Concepts of Positive Horse Training

1. The Comfort Zone
2. The Learning Zone
3. The Reward Cycle
4. The Reward Toolbox
5. Combat Training
6. Trust Builders
7. Trust Busters

Who Can Be an Effective (Human) Trainer?

What are the roles and responsibilities of the human as herd leader? To understand how to communicate confidence and leadership in the horse's language and build a trusting, positive relationship, a trainer needs to cultivate these key characteristics.

- **Emotional Traits**

  Excellent observation skills, to clearly identify different equine responses and understand your horse's needs and motivations

  The ability to project calmness and confidence

  An even temperament and excellent self-control

  A willingness to be still and trust your horse

  Patience and persistence

- **Physical Traits**

  Agility and lightness in weight and movement (there's an old cavalry maxim: Rider and gear should *never* weigh more than 20 percent of the horse's weight!)

  The ability to move slowly and quietly

  Sufficient knowledge, skill, balance, muscle strength, and physical self-control to use correct body language and apply the aids clearly, quickly, and independently

  Sufficient strength and confidence to convince the horse that you *could* back up your requests with a physical threat, if necessary

- **Psychological Traits**

  The ability to plan deliberate actions and alternatives

  The wisdom to recognize when plans and approaches have to change

  The willingness to be a lifelong learner

The Nature of Rewards

It's obvious that the more tools we have in our rewards toolbox, the better. Whether you're leading, longeing, driving, riding, or directing your loose horse from a distance, you need a variety of ways to communicate yes and no.

Not every reward is appropriate for every situation, and not every horse responds to a reward the same way, so you'll need to match the reward to the individual horse and the training environment, as well as to the size and nature of the request.

For example, a food reward can be useful in training a horse to load himself into a trailer or come when called in the pasture, but it isn't appropriate for teaching him to lengthen his stride at the trot. If you're at a show, obviously you can't stop in the middle of an obstacles class to feed your horse a carrot or let him roll in the sand. You can't use your voice to praise your horse in the middle of a dressage test, nor can you turn him loose to let him roll when the farrier still has two more feet to trim. A sensitive mare might really appreciate the softening of a light leg aid, while her coldblooded stablemate might not even notice such a subtle change.

As you consider which rewards will work best in which situations, remember to think about both primary and secondary rewards.

Primary Rewards

Primary rewards speak directly to the horse's basic needs for comfort, balance, and security. They include:

- Releasing pressure (loosening the rein, lightening the leg, taking away the restraint, stopping a push)
- Reducing anxiety (removing a fearful object or situation, restoring security)
- Restoring physical balance (or decreasing imbalance)
- Comforting touches, rubs, and scratches (reminders of grooming-buddy activities)
- Rest and relaxation (lasting only a moment or much longer)
- Unsaddling and removing snug, sweaty, uncomfortable tack
- Freedom (a roll in the sand, a return to his stall or pasture)
- Companionship (your friendship may be just as important as that of his stablemates)
- Food (regular meals, hand grazing, or treats)
- Fun (jumping, splashing in a stream, a trail ride)
- Feelings of strength and well-being from endorphins released during exercise

Trust Busting through Unintentional Threats

I once sold a nice mare to a nice woman; it was a terrible match.

The mare, Billie, was a roan Appaloosa with some Thoroughbred in her ancestry. I'd started her on western, then switched to hunt seat because she'd shown some talent in jumping. She was a sensitive, willing horse, steady on the trails and reliable in the show ring. I thought I'd found the perfect home for her with Marie, a knowledgeable, older woman who'd managed a boarding stable and trained western pleasure horses several years earlier. Marie saw Billie at a local show, fell in love with her, and felt the mare would fit perfectly into her plans to do a little trail riding and breed a few mares.

After Billie passed the vet inspection, Marie arrived with a trailer and a check. Her daughter hopped on Billie bareback, cantered her around the ring, and pronounced her "sweet," so they took her home.

A week later, Marie called and said she was having problems with Billie and would I come help her figure the horse out. For some reason, the mare had become "wild and unmanageable."

When I watched her handling Billie, my heart sank. In only a few days, Billie had changed from a willing, sensitive horse to a fearful, unpredictable one—and it was all because of Marie's body language. The woman's movements were overly energetic, jerky, and unpredictable. Her voice was loud, and even her pats and caresses were rough and quick. She used the rubber curry brush too roughly and in the wrong places. She yanked on the lead rope, abruptly dropped the mare's feet after cleaning them, and asked the horse to move over by shoving abruptly on her hip.

From Billie's point of view, Marie was issuing a constant barrage of threats that the horse couldn't understand.

I gently suggested that Marie might want to slow down and move more quietly around her new horse, but I don't think she understood. Marie confessed that she was nervous because Billie moved quickly and unpredictably,

Secondary Rewards

These indicate the approval of the leader—you. They include:

- Your praising voice
- Your relaxed body language
- Your gestures of approval
- Removing your threat gesture
- Any other neutral signal that is connected to a primary need, such as the sound of a clicker or the sound of a treat being unwrapped

and Billie was nervous because Marie was loud and moved quickly, which made Marie more nervous. . . .

Nervous or not, Marie was determined to saddle up and ride. After she climbed on Billie, she spent a good five minutes shifting around to adjust things: yanking the saddle sideways to center it, kicking her feet around in the stirrups, and flinging the ends of her reins up into the air to untangle them from the saddle horn. Billie fidgeted and danced, so Marie slapped the mare's neck and shouted, "Whoa!" at which point poor Billie shifted from general anxiety into a state of trembling high alert, ready to bolt for any available escape route. I was ready to join her—Marie's fussing and fidgeting and poking and jerking made me almost as nervous as the horse.

This had to be stopped before someone got hurt. I stepped next to Billie and asked Marie to simply drop the reins, *be quiet and sit still*. She found it nearly impossible at first—she confessed that she didn't trust the horse to stand still—but, to her credit, she complied. The mare heaved a big sigh of relief and dropped her head into my arms.

I spent almost two hours explaining to Marie how she was communicating all the wrong things to Billie and why neither one was able to trust the other. I demonstrated how she could change her movements into slower, gentler, more predictable actions that would build trust instead of destroying it. Once Marie was able to understand how frightening and confusing her movements were from Billie's point of view, she could begin to learn more effective methods of communication. We scheduled a month of training and trust-building sessions for Marie and Billie, focusing on groundwork and basic horse-human communication skills. Eventually, they were able to trust each other, and both could enjoy their trail rides.

Your horse should also gain additional, long-term benefits from good training—increased balance, strength, and stamina—which may result in higher status in his equine herd, but it's doubtful that he's able to connect these results with your training activities.

The Six Most Important Rewards in Your Toolbox
To be effective, a reward must be:

- Desirable to the horse
- Closely related in time and place to the specific desired behavior
- Clearly connected to the person who requested the behavior
- Easy for the trainer to give or withhold in almost any situation

Colin McIver

If you can fill the role of a grooming buddy and find the itches that need scratching, you'll have a powerful tool in your rewards toolbox. Combine this with an approving voice, and look for opportunities to reward frequently so that your horse will try harder to gain your approval.

Although you may find yourself using all of the tools in your toolbox at various times, there are six rewards that clearly meet these criteria and are therefore particularly useful in the training process. They are:

1. A comforting touch
2. An approving voice
3. Release of pressure
4. Reduction of anxiety
5. Restoration of balance
6. Rest and relaxation

Savvy trainers usually use two or more of these rewards together, so the horse gains additional feedback for correct responses.

When would you use these rewards? Whenever you can, in as many combinations as will work, *immediately* after the horse gives a correct response. For instance, to ask a dressage horse to lengthen his stride in the trot, first you help him rebalance with leg, seat, and hand aids (half-halt) to prepare for the lengthening. If you ask correctly and he responds correctly, you've helped him acquire balance (the first reward, restoration of balance). You then lighten the hand (the second reward, release of pressure) and keep the legs and seat active to ask for a longer stride.

When he responds, you stop pushing (the third reward, release of pressure again), then half-halt briefly to rebalance again (the fourth reward, balance) and let him come back into his medium trot (the fifth reward, a little rest from the extra exertion). Finally, you let him walk on a loose rein and stretch while you pat and rub his withers and tell him what a fabulous horse he is (lots of rewards: rest, release of pressure, voice, touch, perhaps reduction of anxiety, and restoration of balance).

In competition, you can't use your voice in the arena—but you've still got all those other tools in your toolbox.

What Is *Not* a Reward?

Touch and voice can both be used either as rewards or reprimands. And release of pressure can be confusing to a young horse who may have become accustomed to working on steady contact with constant communication. These actions are *not* rewards from the horse's point of view:

- **Hard, thumping slaps on his neck, ribs, or hindquarters.** Some riders seem to think horses like to be pounded hard, especially after an exciting jump-off or fast calf-roping run. Although some horses will grow to tolerate this behavior, it's much too rough for them to consider it a reward. Remember that a horse's skin is so sensitive and filled with nerve endings

Who Can Give Permission?

Sharon had been successfully showing trained horses for several years on the western pleasure circuit when she decided to purchase her first youngster and finish his training herself. Her horse was a nicely bred 3-year-old Quarter Horse gelding with a friendly eye, but he was also a big, strong fellow with a powerful neck and shoulders. He was doing well under saddle, she told me, and his barn manners were generally quite good—with one serious exception. He'd developed the bad habit of diving into the grass and snatching mouthfuls every time she tried to lead him across the yard to his paddock, where he was turned out daily. She'd nicknamed him Bulldog.

Bulldog had come to Sharon with good ground manners, but he'd begun taking advantage of her when she started to let him hand graze sometimes on the way to the paddock. She now felt the only way she could control him was to run a chain lead over his nose and be prepared to pull hard when he went for the grass. This only seemed to make things worse, however, because recently Bulldog had begun to jig and dance on the lead, alternately flipping his head up or plunging his head down to grab grass in spite of her pulls on the chain.

I wasn't able to watch Sharon and Bulldog in action, so I asked her to explain exactly how she was using the chain lead to correct Bulldog when he wanted to eat but she wanted him to keep walking. "I use a hard, steady pull on the chain to get his head up, then try to haul him along and stay out of the grass," she said.

"What's his reward when he does pick his head up and walk along with you?"

"What do you mean, reward?"

"Do you release the pressure so he knows he's done the right thing?"

"Well, no. I have to keep pulling so he doesn't dive into the grass again."

I explained to Sharon that the first problem was that Bulldog didn't respect her as the leader. Her long, steady pulls on the chain lead weren't an effective correction; they were just teaching Bulldog that he could outpull her—something we don't ever want the horse to know! Her second problem was that she wasn't giving any clear signals to tell him when he'd responded correctly—there was no release of pressure and therefore no reward. He didn't trust her to reliably communicate her commands—he never heard a reliable yes or no—so he was taking on the job of decision making for himself and ignoring her.

I told Sharon that she needed to get away from the grass and spend several sessions reviewing her basic leading techniques to gain Bulldog's focus and respect. She needed to:

- Ask clearly (light tug on the lead, light tap on the hindquarters with a whip if needed) for the correct behavior (walking forward).

- Provide a reward (release the pressure, remove the whip, give a pat or verbal praise) for the correct behavior.

- Apply a quick, *sharp* correction with an immediate release (a sharp jerk on the lead and/or a sharp tap with the whip) when he behaves inappropriately (stopping or lagging behind, twisting to the side, reaching down).

- Provide a reward the *instant* he stops the incorrect behavior.

- Clearly ask again for the correct behavior.

Sharon promised she would go back to the basics to relearn leading at the walk at different speeds, jogging, halting, turning, and backing. Everything must be clear and consistent, and she must never, *ever* get in a tug-of-war that would teach the horse he might win.

Then I asked another question: "Since you're letting him graze on the lead sometimes, how do you tell him when he has permission to eat?"

Sharon was silent for a few seconds. "Um, what do you mean?"

"How does Bulldog know when it's okay for him to graze?"

"Well, I don't pull on the chain or yell at him. So that should tell him."

Poor Bulldog! He had no idea when it was okay for him to graze and when it wasn't. He couldn't trust Sharon because her response to his attempts at grazing were completely random. Bulldog was probably thinking, "Last time I got the grass easily, but this time I had to fight a little to get it. I'll try again and see what happens." Since he couldn't figure out how to please Sharon, he'd developed his own definition of success. Grabbing that grass had become his all-consuming goal.

Since Sharon's first needs were to gain control, reestablish respect, and remain safe, I recommended that she spend at least two weeks on repairing Bulldog's manners and not letting him graze at all while he was being led to the paddock. She should carry a dressage whip in her left hand and use the chain over his nose correctly, being sure corrections were applied sharply and swiftly but that the chain would remain slack when there were no commands or corrections to be applied. She should walk briskly along, looking ahead and using her body language to tell Bulldog where she intended to lead him. If he lagged behind, she should not stop and stare at him or get into a tug-of-war but instead reach back with the whip to tap his hindquarters and remind him to *move forward*. Whenever he tried to go for the grass, she should apply clear, prompt corrections: a quick jerk on the chain and the sharp verbal command "quit!" followed by an immediate release and verbal praise when he complied and the command to keep moving forward. She must be quick, fair and consistent, confident and relaxed, and ready to repeat the request-response-correction-response-reward cycle many, many times.

(continued)

After she was certain that Bulldog would lead obediently even when there was grass within reach, Sharon had a choice to make. She could decide to never, ever let her horse eat grass while on a lead, as some people do, or she could teach him a new command: "Put your head down and eat."

"Instead of letting him guess and become anxious and maybe get it wrong, you need to tell him precisely when you *want* him to stop and eat grass," I explained. "Develop a consistent signal that makes sense to both you and the horse. Have him halt, then touch his muzzle, say 'Okay,' and swing your arm down toward the ground in a little bow. Stand by his shoulder, relax, rub his withers, and move with him as another horse might. Don't challenge him by standing in front or in leading position near his head. Let him decide where to go and what grass to eat.

"When you want to tell him to stop grazing, bring his head up with a quick tug, not a hard steady pull, and immediately walk forward decisively in leading position. You've clearly told him when it's time to graze, and now you're clearly telling him it's time to walk forward. When your horse is on a lead, permission to graze is something *you give to him*, not something *he takes from you*."

Sharon promised to work on her communication skills with Bulldog. She called a few weeks later to report, happily, that Bulldog had reformed— and so had she. She'd had only two major battles with him during the correction phase of his retraining, and they had moved successfully on to the permission-to-graze communication. She no longer needed the chain to manage him.

Eventually, as Sharon and Bulldog became more familiar with each other and she gained his trust as well as his respect, their communications became subtler. Sharon tried to remain clear and consistent in her requests and praise, and Bulldog became more successful at reading her body language. About six months after her original call, Sharon told me that she'd started calling him Willy because his manners had improved to the point where "Bulldog just doesn't fit anymore."

that he can feel a small fly land anywhere on his body. He would be far happier if you gave his withers a quiet scratching than if you smacked his neck or rump. And if that's your way of saying "good job!" what kind of touch can you use as a reprimand if he barges into you or threatens to nip? You've already desensitized him to a sharp slap. (See chapter 6 for a discussion of reward touches and how to develop them.)

- **A loud, excited voice.** When you finally get around that first two-foot hunter course on your green horse, do *not* yell "yahoo!" as you complete your final circle. Your horse will think something bad or frightening has happened to make you raise your voice so sharply. Keep your approval voice quiet and direct it clearly to him so that he fully understands how proud you are of his performance.

- **Overwork.** A good workout can make us all feel good, but many willing, energetic, good-natured horses simply go on and on, never letting on how tired and uncomfortable they're becoming. The trainer, meanwhile, is delighted because of the horse's fast progress. But if you work your horse until he's sore, he'll have to figure out how to make himself feel more comfortable. That often means stiffness and resistance, which means he's going to shut down the learning process so he can protect himself.

Remember, if your horse cannot rely on you for rest, reward, safety, and comfort, he will find ways to get what he needs without you. He'll elect himself leader instead, and he won't continue to learn from you.

Every moment counts, and horses have very long memories. You don't get to throw away a few unproductive hours, nor can you ever apologize to the horse for betraying his trust. If you ask your horse to cross a river, you'd better know that the crossing is safe or be ready to trust his expert judgment about what's underfoot. If your horse gets stuck in quicksand or becomes trapped between submerged boulders, you've destroyed part of his trust in you. He may never again trust you, at least not when it comes to crossing an unknown river. You've failed to perform as a leader worthy of his trust.

Make the Connection to Time, Place, and Behavior

A reward isn't a reward unless it's immediately connected to the response. Ten seconds later may be too late; thirty seconds later is definitely too late.

Giving your horse a carrot when you put him back in his pasture is *not* a reward for the good ride you finished half an hour earlier. It can't be because, although the carrot brings the horse pleasure and he will certainly associate it with the person who offers it, it's not clearly connected to the general activity of riding. Horses live in the present, so your horse will connect the carrot to whatever he happens to be doing when the carrot appears—rubbing his face on your shoulder, tugging on the halter, pawing the ground, or standing on your foot.

Remember, too, that from the horse's point of view, being allowed to stop and rest at the end of the ride is the best reward he can receive and one he clearly understands. So, you've already provided a very good reward by dismounting and loosening the girth.

Richard Valcourt

Food can be a useful motivator in training, but ultimately you'll want your horse to seek a higher reward—his leader's praise and approval. Meredith is giving Coosa Lani three rewards: a quiet voice of approval, a light scratch on the withers, and an opportunity to stretch and relax.

If you want to give him a carrot at the end of a good ride because it makes *you* feel good, that's fine, but try to connect the carrot to a specific request so that you're not ignoring a training opportunity. For example, you can ask him to walk politely through the gate and stand quietly while you remove his halter. *Then* give the carrot as a reward for a specific good behavior.

4

SETTING AND MEETING
YOUR TRAINING GOALS

To be a useful, valued member of our equestrian society, every horse should have at least a basic education that is based on trust in his human leaders. When a horse offers his trust to a human, he is willingly submitting to that human. Willing submission is *not* the same as slavery, and it is never based on coercion or pain; rather, it's voluntarily giving up control to a leader who is firm, confident, and absolutely worthy of the horse's trust.

The level of education and cooperation that's required of a horse will vary, of course, with the role we've assigned to the horse: a broodmare, for instance, may be required only to demonstrate good manners and a willingness to cooperate while being handled, bred, transported, and examined. A successful cutting horse, on the other hand, must be adept at simultaneously interpreting subtle signals from his rider and the cattle he's working, while rapidly transferring trust and complex decision-making skills back and forth between himself and his rider.

We owe it to our horses to give them the best education possible, so our horses will have a good chance of success in all aspects of their relationships with humans. That *best education* is based on trust and respect.

The Five Principles of Setting Goals

You can't go forward if you don't know where you want to go. First establish your goals; then create a step-by-step program that will help you achieve them. No matter what your riding discipline, there are five basic principles to follow as you decide what you and your horse should be achieving:

1. Get the basics down first. Don't even think of asking your horse to jump or learn reining patterns or negotiate tough trail obstacles if his basic flatwork isn't confirmed. Your horse should be rhythmic, forward, straight, and willing and balanced in all his gaits, through turns and on straight lines, both inside and outside the arena—*before* you ask for more advanced work.

2. Don't pigeonhole your horse. Just because he's bred to be a Grand Prix dressage competitor doesn't mean he'll enjoy it or even that he'll be good at it. Let your horse tell you what he finds rewarding.

3. Set manageable goals and reward the process, not just the end product. Training is incremental. It takes *time* and *repetition*. You can't just push a button and produce a national champion.

4. Be broad-minded and consider how your horse's new skills might be adapted for other riding disciplines. Be willing to consider different methods for achieving your goals.

5. Understand that you and your horse are lifelong learners. Read, watch, listen, and learn from other disciplines as well as your own. Seek to learn new skills so you can always improve your communication with all your horses as you help them learn to find rewarding ways of working for you.

Where to Train

Despite what real estate agents will tell you, location isn't everything. Of course, it would be nice to have the perfect training environment. My ideal training facility would include a 20-by-60-meter dressage arena, a 200-by-400-foot covered arena with mirrors, lots of different jumps and cavalletti for gymnastic jumping, a half-mile racetrack for gallops and distance work, a 60-foot-diameter round pen, a separate small arena with trail obstacles, a cross-country jump course with hills and streams, and about 50 miles of interesting trails over varied terrain. It would all have perfect footing, of course, and be located next to the ocean so we could ride on the sand and swim in the surf. That would be nice, but I've never come even close to that kind of setup, and most of us have to settle for far less.

Your basic training area needs to be large enough so your horse can walk, trot, and canter freely, in both straight lines and turns. The footing should be relatively level, free of rocks, and soft enough to provide cushioning but not so soft and deep that your horse has to struggle and become exhausted after twenty minutes of exertion. Five inches of coarse sand over a firm base is about right; fine sand can get too dusty, and coarser material can cause bruising. Shredded rubber, bark, or a commercially prepared surface material designed specifically for arenas can also work well, but only if the base provides good drainage. Bark may produce mold and rot, and rubber can be slippery in wet climates, but both of these are fine if you have the luxury of a covered or indoor arena.

A 60-foot-diameter round pen can be very useful for starting young horses or green riders, helping horses develop balance on a trot or canter circle, and helping a rider develop her seat with no-reins and no-stirrups exercises. But the round pen should not be your only training area, and it isn't absolutely necessary to have one. The round pen and its comforting curved fence line can easily become a crutch for both horses and riders. Horses who have been worked exclusively in round pens often appear lost when they're ridden in an area with long straightaways and no wall to travel next to. And riders often discover their skills aren't as good as they thought when they take on full responsibility for balancing and directing their horses out in the open.

If I have to choose between a round pen and a larger rectangular arena for training, I'll choose the rectangular arena every time. Being able to ride corners, straight lines, and serpentines is far more valuable than simply going around in the same circle track all the time. However, if I'm working a young horse in a large, open space, I will often begin by using barrels and poles to block off a smaller space—perhaps a 60-by-80-foot rectangle—to reduce distractions, clearly define our training area, and keep my green horse's attention focused on me. Regardless of the area's size, I don't want a solid-walled enclosure that my horse and I can't see out of. Horses become concerned about what's lurking behind the wall, especially if there's a strange noise or activity going on just out of view. It's better to learn how to deal with the occasional distraction than to train your horse in a walled enclosure.

To teach a new task, you need to take your horse through three stages of learning: *introduction*, *reinforcement*, and *confirmation*. During the *introduction* phase, you'll want the fewest distractions possible so your horse can focus on you without other people or animals drawing away his attention. Try to introduce a new skill when nothing much is happening around the barn—early on a Sunday morning, for instance, or at lunchtime during the workweek.

When you are *reinforcing* a newly learned task, you and your horse should be able to manage minor distractions, including the normal activity of the familiar barn and training area.

To *confirm* the training, you'll go away from home base and duplicate the new skills at a show, out on the trails, or at a friend's less-familiar arena. When your horse can perform calmly and obediently with lots of distractions all around him, then you'll know the training is solid, and you won't have to excuse his inattention or bad manners by saying, "But he does this perfectly at home!"

First, Master the Basics

Whether your horse is a green youngster or has been under saddle for some time, it's important to establish certain benchmarks in your horse's education—and maybe provide a refresher course, if needed. *All* horses over the age of weaning should:

- Lead well at the walk and trot. This means the horse travels with his head even with your shoulder, speeding up when you go faster, slowing down when you slow down, and stopping when you stop—all with just occasional light pressure, or no pressure, on a conventional halter and lead rope. The horse should pause to let you go first through gates and doorways, follow willingly when asked to go away from the barn or his friends, and turn easily in a tight circle. You should be able to lead him easily and comfortably from *both* sides.

- Stand quietly in a halter when tied with a single rope or in crossties.

- Move his hindquarters or shoulders to the side when directed, and step back straight and willingly when asked.

- Pick up any foot and stand calmly for trimming or shoeing without kicking, pulling away, or leaning on his handler.

- Load and travel quietly in a trailer or van—alone, with a buddy, or with an unfamiliar horse.

- Be easy to catch and halter in the field or paddock.

- Lower his head to be haltered or bridled.

- Stand quietly for trimming, clipping, and bathing.

- Walk willingly through water and over different surfaces, such as plywood or a tarp.

- Calmly accept all the sights and sounds commonly found in a stable: hissing fly repellent, a crackling bug zapper, the ripping sound of Velcro being unfastened, tools clattering in a wheelbarrow, blankets being shaken and draped over a fence, electric drill or staple-gun noises, a hose being pulled along the ground, plastic and paper bags rustling, and so on.

- Walk quietly past or stand calmly near moving cars, motorcycles, bicycles, dogs, cows, goats, and motorized farm equipment.

      No matter what his age, if your horse is lacking some of these basic skills, review the progressive exercises in Part II to see which areas you need to work on. The basic groundwork in chapters 6 and 7, plus the combat training work in chapter 14, will help your horse build patterns of obedience and acceptance.

      Look for opportunities to introduce your horse to something new or different. If a friend has purchased a new motorbike, or the farmer down the road has brought in a new herd of goats, or neighbors have set up a tent in their backyard, consider yourself fortunate! Those are all opportunities for training, not fearful situations to be avoided. As a trainer, you have a responsibility to introduce your horse to as many new and challenging situations as possible. If you can add these new items to his repertoire in a relaxed, confident fashion, you'll build obedience, respect, and trust.

Round Pen Work

When done correctly, round pen work can be a very effective technique for establishing respect and obedience in a horse of almost any age. Essentially, you're using the limited area of a round pen to establish control—while still on the ground—over the horse's speed, direction, and mental focus, just as a lead horse would do in a herd. By driving a horse forward, directing his responses, inviting the horse to approach you submissively, and then rewarding him by removing the pressure, you can teach him to pay close attention to your body language, voice, and gestures.

However, when round penning is done incorrectly—chasing the horse wildly with a whip or rope so he runs in fear, making him run until he's exhausted and defeated, or causing him to stop or turn by flinging dirt or a rope in his face—all you create is a fearful, tense horse who flinches at every gesture. The true goal in round penning is to create a subtle system of communication from the ground and fine-tune your horse's ability to pay careful attention to you, the all-important leader. Although aggressive round pen work can be very effective for establishing control over strong, dominant horses, it can also turn more fearful horses into nervous, hyper-alert animals who are constantly seeking escape, not cooperation.

Many good books have been written about round penning. Richard Shrake, Monty Roberts, John Lyons, and others have all explained their training techniques in careful detail, so I won't attempt to duplicate their work here.

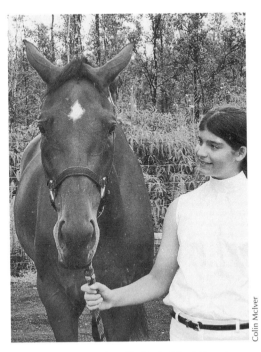

Willa is 17 hands tall; Rachel is 5-foot-4. Rachel needs her mare to put her head down on command, so she applies simple, steady pressure on the poll . . .

. . . and rewards Willa immediately with a release and a word of praise when the mare drops her head. Clicker training and food rewards also work well for this exercise.

Longeing

Quite frankly, if I have to choose between round penning and longeing, I'd rather use the longe line. The same patterns of attention, obedience, and submission that round penning seeks to establish can also be accomplished on the longe line, without building an extra training area. And longeing can help you do so much more than round penning: You can establish the horse's rhythm in all gaits, adjust his length of stride, and improve his balance on straight lines as well as circles of various sizes. If you're working with a very large, very ungainly young horse, a 70-foot or even an 80-foot round pen isn't going to be large enough to let him find his balance on a canter circle. On the longe, however, you can easily vary the size of your circle, moving from very large to quite small depending on your horse's needs. And if you're working in an arena with square corners and straight sides, you can use those barriers to help you slow, stop, block, or encourage your horse.

I know of at least one trainer who believes longeing is of very little value. "What's the point in forcing your horse to go around and around in boring drill work, jammed into a fake balance with tight sidereins and no relief?" she says. "That just numbs his brain and teaches a horse to resent the work!" I'd have to agree because the way she describes longeing sounds pretty horrible.

But when done correctly, longeing is an invaluable part of almost every stage of training for horse and rider. For the rider, mounted longeing without stirrups or reins helps strengthen balance and create an independent seat, legs, and hands. For the horse, unmounted longeing can help you:

- Develop the horse's topline, back, and hindquarter muscles.
- Teach your horse to manage smooth gait transitions (especially trot-canter and canter-trot) without the interference of a rider.
- Encourage contact with and acceptance of the bit.
- Improve cadence, rhythm, and regularity.
- Teach obedience to gestures and voice commands.
- Improve your horse's balance on circles of various sizes.

Once you've established patterns of control and obedience on the longe line, you can use those skills in many other ways: to warm up or help settle a fresh horse, to help develop a rider's balance and independent aids, to introduce your horse to cavalletti or small jumps, to teach him to lengthen and shorten his stride, to watch your horse move under new tack, to present a horse to a prospective buyer, or to demonstrate lameness for a veterinarian.

Longeing Equipment

Your longeing equipment should consist of a comfortable longe line (preferably cotton or soft nylon), gloves, a longe whip, a surcingle or saddle, protective boots for your horse, elastic sidereins or sliding sidereins, and a snug halter or simple snaffle bridle (depending on the horse's level of training). Some trainers insist on a longeing cavesson, but I feel the pressure and leverage that a cavesson places on the bridge of a horse's nose isn't particularly helpful because it's easy to pull a horse off balance by tugging on the front of his face. I've also seen several horses get loose in less-than-optimal circumstances when the front ring on an inexpensive longe cavesson broke off.

To longe with a halter, simply attach the longe line to the inside halter ring and make sure the halter fits snugly so the cheekpiece won't be pulled into the horse's outside eye if you have to put some pressure on the longe line to bring him under control. If you find that your horse is too strong or playful for you to control on the longe with just a plain halter, you can thread a longe line with a chain over the noseband (as shown in the photo on page 74), but don't use a chain unless you absolutely must to gain his attention, and get rid of the chain as soon as you can trust your horse to travel sensibly on the longe and listen to your commands.

Work on a longe line is *training*, not a substitute for regular turnout. You can expect a young, green, or fresh horse to be a little exuberant on the longe at first, but if you make a habit of letting your horse run around wildly on the longe, kicking and bucking and generally disregarding your commands, or if you actively encourage him to run wildly on the longe to help him let off steam, you're teaching him that even though he's all tacked up and you're pretending to be in control, he can ignore you and do whatever he pleases.

Coosa Lani is ready for longeing, with the reins caught up in the throatlatch, the stirrups tied up, and sidereins attached to her snaffle bit at a comfortable length and height.

To attach the longe line to a snaffle bit, simply clip it to the inside bit ring. If your horse tends to get strong and pull on the longe, run the line through the inside bit ring and up over his poll, and clip it to the outside bit ring. If you leave the reins on your bridle, twist them under his neck a few times and thread the throatlatch through a loop of reins to keep them safely up away from his feet.

If you're longeing with an English saddle, remove the stirrups or keep them from banging your horse's sides by tying a snug knot in the leathers and clipping a short piece of twine or leather to both irons so they stay up and out of the way. If your horse is wearing a western saddle, use a small piece of twine or a shoelace to tie each stirrup snugly to the cinch. Although every horse needs to learn to accept flopping stirrups calmly, without bucking or panicking, having stirrups bang into his ribs at every stride when you're longeing to develop balance or prompt transitions does *not* promote a sensitive response to your leg aids.

Always use protective boots on your horse's front legs. Hind boots are also a very good idea if your horse is young, green, clumsy, or travels close behind.

Attach elastic-fixed sidereins or sliding sidereins from the bit to the girth so that your horse has light, even contact on both sidereins when his head is just in front of the vertical. Keep them a couple of inches longer for a green or young horse, and always adjust sidereins so they are longer for work at the walk, shorter for the trot and canter. You may have to adjust the length of the sidereins several times during the course of a longeing session, depending on your work plan and your horse's responses.

Why use sidereins? They support your horse, encourage him to stay straight, help him connect his back end to his front end by encouraging him to lower his head and use his back muscles properly, and teach him to accept steady rein contact through transitions. They also make it harder for the exuberant horse to buck, kick, or bolt.

Sliding Sidereins

Although we'd all love to have our horses develop good balance and correct muscling with very little help from us, it just doesn't happen. They simply aren't designed to carry riders or pull loads. To make these tasks easier and more pleasant for your horse, you need to teach him to lower his head and neck as he learns to accept the bit, engage his hindquarters, and develop his pushing ability.

Correctly used sliding sidereins can help.

Sliding sidereins were first developed and used by a German trainer who was looking for a way to help his young horses find their balance on the flat before they went on to jumping. Not every horse needs or will benefit from sliding sidereins, but in many cases they can dramatically encourage a young or badly trained horse, or one with poor conformation, to learn balance and strength without allowing him to travel *upside down* (that is, hollow-backed, above the bit and against the rider's hands).

Sliding sidereins consist of a single long rein or rope that attaches to a midpoint D-ring on the left side of the surcingle or girth, passes through the left ring of the snaffle bit, then runs down between the horse's front legs to the D-ring at the middle of the girth and back up to the right ring of the snaffle bit, and attaches to the right-side D-ring on the surcingle or girth. The length can be adjusted by tightening or loosening either side of the continuous rein at the side of the girth or surcingle.

To work properly, sliding sidereins *must* be able to slide freely through the bit rings and through the D-ring at the center of the girth or surcingle—hence the name. Sliding sidereins have several advantages over fixed sidereins:

- As the horse bends into a turn, the continuous sliding sidereins conform to the horse's lateral bend, adjusting in tension and supporting either a left or a right bend.

- Because of the limiting pressure from the lower portion of the sliding sidereins, horses cannot get above the bit as they can with traditional sidereins.

- When the horse is using his back and neck muscles correctly—stretching his topline and stepping forward with his hind legs engaged—the sliding sidereins place no additional pressure on the horse, so the reward is immediate.

Emily is working hard to push Taser energetically forward into a stretched, lengthened trot. Because Taser can be a bit exuberant on the longe, the longe line is passed through the snaffle bit ring on the near side and clipped to the bit on the far side. Note the sliding sidereins, which invite the horse to stretch long and low.

- Sliding sidereins give the horse a continuous invitation to stretch long and low. Fixed sidereins, on the other hand, don't allow the desirable long-and-low frame.

- At the walk, sliding sidereins adjust to the telescoping motion of the horse's head and neck by sliding left-right, left-right.

- Because of the "live" feel that sliding sidereins give to the horse, horses who fret in fixed sidereins often do well in sliding sidereins.

Although they appear similar to sliding sidereins, Vienna longe reins are not the same. Vienna longe reins are not continuous, so they must be separately adjusted for length, and they do not automatically slide to change the tension on both sides when the horse bends laterally.

If your horse carries his head severely to one side when traveling on the longe or being ridden, you may have to fix the sliding rein at the girth so that it cannot slide freely. Be sure both sides are then exactly the same length to help your horse go straight.

Note that some horses can panic if they feel *any* restriction on their head. Always start with sidereins a little loose, then tighten gradually. And always work first on the longe before climbing on a horse wearing any kind of restrictive device or auxiliary rein.

The Longe Whip

Always use a good, lightweight longe whip, *not* a coiled rope or the end of the longe line to send your horse forward. The whip is an important extension of your arm, and your gestures must be precise and consistent for effective communication. Devotees of the round pen will often fling a coiled rope at a loose horse to move him forward, but in longeing you want precise, controlled communication with your horse, not rapid, uncontrolled flight. You cannot toss or twirl a rope with anything close to the precision of a whip. Besides, if you later need to toss a rope over something close to your horse—a cow, a gatepost, another horse—you don't want him flinching and rushing away at the sight of a rope sailing through the air.

The whip is not an instrument of punishment. Use it to direct the horse forward and away from you, not to invoke fear. You can point it, wiggle it, or gently snap the lash near the ground to get his attention if he's sluggish. If he's a little dull to the subtleties of a wiggling whip, you can poke, prod, or tap, but you may not touch a horse with anything more than a tap, except in self-defense or to correct aggressive, violent behavior such as kicking.

Develop your expertise in handling the longe line and whip. As with any skill, training on the longe requires practice on the part of the trainer. To be effective, you need to coordinate line, whip, gestures, voice, body posture, and position relative to the horse's position and movement. If you wave the whip threateningly when you don't really mean to, if you get ahead of your horse so

Bunny, a 17-year-old Quarter Horse mare with very straight shoulders and hocks, spent several years learning how to avoid pain from harsh hands and severe curb bits. Her response to any rein contact, even with a mild snaffle bit and Holly's quiet, tactful riding, is to tense her back and fling her head into the air.

An easy, effective, and kind solution for Bunny's problem is to work in sliding sidereins, which discourage her head-up, back-hollow evasions while inviting a stretched topline. Here she's accepting the bit, working through her back, and engaging her hindquarters about as much as her conformation allows. Note that the sliding sidereins are quite slack; simply knowing that they're there is enough to help Bunny respond well to Holly's request for quiet, elastic contact.

he stops in confusion, if you or your horse get wound up in the line or trip, someone's going to get upset or hurt. Practice gathering, paying out, and taking in the line with either hand leading; take the longe whip out behind the barn where you won't disturb anyone, and practice flicking it at objects until you're comfortable carrying, pointing, raising, lowering, wiggling, snapping, flicking, and dropping it with either hand.

As with all things connected with horses, your goal is to be clear, precise, and only as firm as necessary; not clumsy, heavy-handed, or confusing to the horse.

Basic Training on the Longe

To begin longeing, start to the left, or counterclockwise. Hold your longe line in your left hand about 6 feet away from your horse. Hold the remainder of the longe line (looped, not coiled) and your whip in your right hand. Point the whip at your horse's left hip, say "walk," and begin walking backward, using the whip in a poking, wiggling, or tapping motion to send him forward and a little away from you. When he complies, keep the whip still but continue pointing at his hindquarters to let him know he's to keep moving. When he pauses, resume the small movements or taps of the whip. As he goes forward more willingly, drop back toward his hindquarters and turn your body toward him so you're facing his hip and he's moving ahead of you. Direct him in a circle around you; your feet should describe a small circle, stepping sideways, as his feet describe a larger circle about 10 feet away. When you can create a good circle at the walk with him about 10 feet away from you, ask him to trot, pay out the line, and see if you can enlarge the circle so he's working in a circle about 50 to 60 feet in diameter.

Horses just starting out on the longe often stop walking forward when you're farther away than your whip can reach, so to enlarge the circle to a reasonable size, you're probably going to have to get him trotting. The momentum of the faster gait will carry him out into the larger circle.

Don't work a green horse at a trot or canter on anything smaller than a 50-foot-diameter circle; the torque (turning stress) on their legs is too great, and their balance is probably too uncertain to make small circles productive. The younger or less fit the horse, the larger the circle must be! Never longe a youngster (2 years or younger) for more than five minutes in each direction, and don't longe in anything smaller than a 60-foot-diameter circle—their joints simply cannot take it.

Use a combination of words and gestures to control your horse's movements. To send him from a walk into a trot, sharply say, "trot!" with a strong upward inflection (troh-*ot!*), move a little back toward his tail, and point or wiggle the whip at his hindquarters. Your subtle threat gestures (abrupt movements, open body stance with square shoulders and outstretched arms, raised whip) should keep him moving forward and away from you.

To slow down to a walk or a halt, say "walk" or "whoa" in a soothing, dropping tone of voice (*wah*-awk or *whoa*-oh), change your position so you're a little in front of his movement, and let the whip drop or trail behind you; in other words, stop chasing him. Use your good-boy reward voice and approval gestures (relaxed body posture, slightly slumped shoulders). Gradually enlarge the circle. (To keep him going consistently forward, at first *you* may have to walk in a fairly large circle, too, so that you can stay within whip's reach of his hindquarters.)

To reverse, first stop him, then change the longe line to the other side of the halter or bridle, and lead him around into the new direction. It's not a good idea to teach a horse to reverse by himself on the longe line, even if you're using a cavesson with a front-of-the-nose attachment; many horses learn to use a sudden reverse as an evasion tactic.

When your horse is calm and obedient on the longe in both directions at walk, trot, and whoa, you can begin asking for different speeds and lengths of stride within each gait. Use slightly different commands ("walk *on*!" or "trot easy") to change speeds within a gait; position several ground poles on the perimeter of your longe circle to encourage him to lengthen stride on a large circle. It's easiest to do this along a fence line or other barrier to help keep your horse traveling straight.

Remember:

- Always wear gloves! Don't risk a rope burn.

- Longe in a confined area, at least for the first few sessions. If your horse gets going too fast or won't listen to a "whoa," you can quickly change your position and push your horse into a corner, a wall, or a fence to stop him.

- Keep longe sessions short—no more than half an hour—and change direction frequently.

- Do *not* get within kicking range of your horse's hind feet! Even if you don't feel you need a longe whip to keep your horse moving, carrying one is a good idea because it gives you an arm extension and pushes the horse out and away from you.

- Coordinate your voice and gestures and be consistent! The voice commands learned on the longe will help you teach your horse obedience and promptness under saddle.

- You are controlling your horse's direction and movement, so you are in charge. Therefore, you *must* give him feedback and tell him when he's done the right thing. Provide lots of rewards; a verbal "good boy!" plus frequent rest breaks will mean a lot to your horse. Add a forehead rub and a pat on the withers every time you approach him to reverse or adjust the tack.

Developing Balance at the Canter on the Longe

One of the best uses of the longe line is to help your horse strengthen his back muscles so he can develop better balance in the canter and in trot-canter transitions, with no interference from a rider.

If you're having problems riding into or out of the canter (if your horse rushes, flings his head up, falls forward, hangs on your hands, leans over his inside shoulder, or just plain has trouble maintaining a smooth, steady canter), don't fight or fuss with him. He may simply not be able to balance himself plus a rider. Put him on the longe and ask for trot-canter transitions. Keep the circles large and the canters brief; give him the chance to come back down to a trot before his canter falls apart. Then calmly reorganize and begin again.

Keep these points in mind:

- If your horse repeatedly rushes or picks up the wrong lead, don't punish him. By remaining calm as you help him find his balance, you'll continue to be his trustworthy adviser. If you lose your temper, you'll lose his trust and respect. Think instead of how you can improve his understanding of what you're asking.

- Try asking him to canter as he's heading along a wall toward a corner. The corner will discourage him from simply running. It will also help him figure out which way he has to go and encourage him to pick up the correct lead. As he approaches the corner, tighten the longe line a little to indicate the direction, then ask for the canter.

- If he rushes madly around at the canter, bring him back to trot, using a fence line or corner to slow him down if necessary.

- If he falls forward into a wild, disorganized trot when you ask him to come down from the canter, immediately ask for the walk so he starts thinking about shifting his weight back onto his haunches more quickly as you go from canter to trot.

- If your horse is able to escape your signals because he's traveling in a very large circle but you know he can't canter on anything smaller, you will have to shorten the longe line and get closer to him while at the same time enlarging your own walking circle so that he can continue traveling in a large circle. This can be exhausting—you'll be loping along sideways pretty vigorously to keep him going between your leading (line) hand and your driving (whip) hand—but it is sometimes necessary to maintain control. The longer your whip, the easier this will be.

- When your horse shows even a small hint of progress or understanding, give him rest and reward! Don't keep drilling, drilling, and drilling just because his response isn't quite perfect.

The Importance of Cross-Training

Cross-training is an excellent way to develop versatility while you keep yourself and your horse fresh. The same principles of balance and communication apply across all riding styles, so if your basic training is sound, you should be able to take any horse onto the trails, ride comfortably over small jumps, perform passably well in the dressage ring, change your tack (from western to hunt seat, saddle seat, or sidesaddle), and even train your horse to drive if you have the space, the equipment, and the desire.

As dressage master Charles deKunffy states in his book, *Training Strategies for Dressage Riders*, "Horses cannot be improved by giving them physical exercises only. The diversification of work awakens the horse's mind. Movement over open country and acquaintance with varied terrain is indispensable to the development of the horse." Also, "The dressage rider has to be, first of all, a horse person who is acquainted with a diversity of equestrian activities, because only by these means can the nature of the horse be discovered. A dressage rider cannot be 'made' by riding dressage only. . . . The bold and powerful gaits of an alert horse negotiating a natural environment cannot be experienced in a fenced-in arena."

Jane Savoie, in her book *Cross-train Your Horse*, says, "There was a time when I thought that I couldn't possibly have anything in common with a rider wearing a cowboy hat. . . . But then, I did some extensive research. I interviewed lots of highly successful trainers from many different fields of riding and discovered that they were all in agreement about two things. They all use basic dressage principles in their training, and they're quick to credit much of their success to the strong foundation provided by it."

So if you and your horse are becoming bored with one style of riding or you think that perhaps you'd both be better suited to a different activity, expand your horizons! Trail riding teaches a horse responsibility about where to step and how to balance himself with minimal direction from his rider; western pleasure riding can encourage a horse to travel slow and low; cavalletti and jumping can strengthen a horse's back and help him learn to lengthen and shorten strides.

Just be sure that each new activity you're exploring follows the basics of being calm, forward, straight, responsive, and balanced. Every discipline has its fringe element, where trainers seem to have forgotten these basic principles of positive training in their pursuit of fads, trophies, and prize money. Some sad results of these extremes include western pleasure horses who were taught to lope so slowly and crookedly that onlookers began referring to the movement as the *cripple crawl*, carriage horses locked into destructive headsets with severe checkreins, and flashy breed classes that rewarded "animation" achieved by terrorizing young horses with whips and fire extinguishers.

5

REHABILITATING
THE PROBLEM HORSE

A responsive, attentive, willing, confident, eager-to-please horse who understands his job and willingly offers respect to his human partner is a joy to work with. Most horses, of course, fall at least a little bit short in one of those characteristics, just as we humans aren't exactly perfect, either.

Then there are those horses who have had such poor relationships with humans that they've abandoned all sense of trust, respect, or obedience. Some of them are simply very sensitive and nervous and have never met a human who could understand them or forge a bond of trust and obedience with them; some horses may have been truly abused; still others have been spoiled by submissive humans, so they've never learned how to accept a trainer's direction.

Experienced riders enjoy riding a well-trained, sensitive horse. This is the horse who anticipates your every request, who is so in tune with his rider that he seems to read your thoughts. But the overly sensitive horse, the horse who overreacts to the smallest stimulus—and often picks the *wrong* reaction—can be a nightmare. These horses often don't need any outside source to cause fear and pain because they frighten or hurt themselves. An overly sensitive horse may leap across his stall and crash into the wall because someone dropped a bucket or another horse snorted.

Other horses have been hurt, abused, or mishandled. Abuse isn't always obvious; sometimes it takes the form of "training." The rider who repeatedly jerks his horse in the mouth as punishment for taking off too early at a jump or uses spurs and a whip to "correct" his green horse for spooking in fear, the "trainer" who tries to desensitize a horse's fears by throwing him on the ground and hitting him with a plastic tarp until the horse freezes in terror, the contestant who ties his horse's head eight feet off the ground on a short lead rope for 20 hours before a show so the horse will "learn" not to carry his head so high in a pleasure class—these people are engaging in abuse just as surely as the callous teamster in *Black Beauty*.

Some horses respond to abuse by simply shutting down or freezing in fear. Others go into a panic, flinging themselves over backward in an effort to get free at whatever cost. Less-sensitive horses may turn stubborn, resistant, or vicious.

Developing Trust in Fearful Horses

An abused horse has a good reason to fear and mistrust humans. But with very careful, consistent, patient handling, most abused horses can learn to trust humans. The overly sensitive horse, on the other hand, may always be limited in the amount of trust and trustworthiness he can attain.

Environmental factors may also affect some horses more than others. Some researchers have suggested that horses might possess *smart bodies*—highly sensitive faculties that help them locate and respond to herd movements, sounds, or electromagnetic fields (similar to the extrasensory abilities of schooling fish and migrating birds). Sensitive horses may react to electrical pulses from underground electrical cables or overhead power lines that we humans aren't aware of. I once owned an otherwise calm mare who would become fearful and agitated every time our trail rides took us underneath high-tension wires; tying her near a utility pole during a lunch break provoked a near disaster. Once her slow-witted human partner figured out the cause of her panic, we moved to a different location and enjoyed a peaceful lunch.

Some horses overreact to electric fencing, refusing to go near anything that looks like a fence wire—perhaps even refusing to go through a narrow gateway bounded by electric fencing. The same mare who had trouble with high-tension wires could be kept reliably in a field fenced with nothing more than baling twine; she'd touched a hot wire once and was thoroughly suspicious of anything that resembled electric fencing.

Regardless of whether the fear is caused by nature or nurture, abused and overreactive horses are perhaps the most difficult to work with. They are driven by fear and pain, or the anticipation of pain. When a horse exhibits concern or fear about a situation, the trainer's responsibility is to reduce the horse's anxiety level and get him safely back into his comfort zone, not to force the issue and provoke a fight. Yelling, hitting, trapping, forcing, or otherwise hurting a horse while he's in a fear state will only confirm his fears. The horse only knows that he was feeling afraid and suspicious and then he got hurt, so now he's *certain* he doesn't ever want to go there or do that again!

Whenever a horse sends out fear signals—high head, tense body, intense concentration in ears and eyes, trembling—you need to reduce the fear by giving him a chance to move away. Find a way to let him step back into his comfort zone, give him time to assess the situation, and then ask again for his cooperation, perhaps at a less-intense level.

When working with an abused and fearful horse:

- Don't provoke panic in an effort to make him face his fears. He can't become confident or courageous until he's learned to trust you, and that's the crux of the problem—he doesn't trust anyone. Instead, practice the ground exercises in chapters 6 and 7 and then very carefully work on the combat training exercises in chapter 14 that he's comfortable with.

- Go right back to the basics, and don't assume anything. Accept the fact that you'll need to spend many, many hours on the ground and in the saddle to gain trust, instill new patterns of obedience, and undo the damage that's been done to an abused, fearful horse.

- Make the daily routine and the training routine monotonous. Don't move on to anything new until the horse is very relaxed with the basics. If you can't bear that much monotony, seek out someone who can.

- Find extra ways to reassure and reward. Fearful horses lack confidence, both in their riders and in their own ability to do something right. Look for even the smallest signs of trust, relaxation, and cooperation and reward them.

- Most frightened horses will feel more comfortable in an enclosed area where they know their limits; others appear claustrophobic and need more space in which to relax. Find out which situation makes your horse feel more at ease.

- Don't move abruptly around an abused or highly sensitive horse, and don't let anyone else move quickly or roughly around him, either. Make every move deliberate, predictable, and a little slow. Don't touch him suddenly or pop out from behind a stall door.

- Talk to him a lot, and help him learn that your voice is positive and soothing.

- Be careful. When a terrified horse needs to get away to feel safe, he's going to move explosively—forward, backward, or over the top of anyone or anything. Even when you feel you're making progress, if he's placed in a stressful situation, he may blow up.

- No matter how hard you try, you may have to make accommodations for his phobias. The fearful horse may never be truly safe to tie, reliable on the trails, or easy to load in a trailer.

Victor's Claustrophobia

Victor is a highly sensitive, very intelligent Thoroughbred gelding who raced for two years on the East Coast. After 42 races, a knee injury ended his career, and I acquired him as a pleasure horse. Two arthroscopic surgeries successfully removed the bone chips from his knee. His physical rehabilitation and reschooling went well, and he became a friendly, responsive pleasure horse with a lumpy knee but no long-term soundness issues.

His former life had left him with another, less-visible scar, however: Victor is severely claustrophobic. He's comfortable inside a stall only if the stall is very large, high ceilinged, and airy; if given the choice, Victor would rather not go into a stall at all. He'd rather stand outside in the worst blizzard imaginable than spend time in a stall with solid, high walls on all four sides. Put his grain in such a stall, and he'll snatch a mouthful and run back outside to chew it.

Needless to say, this presented a problem when he needed to be trailered. Victor's fear of closed spaces may have developed in the starting gate at the racetrack because at first his approach to loading in a trailer was to dance sideways and threaten to rear over backward for at least half an hour. Then he would gather his courage and hurl himself forward into the trailer—and immediately fly out backward again, shaking like a leaf and drenched in sweat. All the approved trailer-loading methods didn't work with this horse. We tried quiet, persistent tapping with a whip (he reared), placing a longe line around his rump (he reared), loading a companion pony first (no interest), placing his food on the ramp or in the trailer (no interest). We tried ramps and step-ups, straight-load trailers and slant-loads, the biggest we could find, with the partitions pushed aside or removed completely.

Every time he saw the trailer parked in the yard, he'd break out in a sweat and begin pacing nervously in his stall or paddock.

Victor's manners on the ground were quite good—he'd walk, stop, back promptly, and keep his head near my shoulder at whatever speed I moved

Handling the Spoiled Horse

To survive and be accepted as a valued member of equine and human society, horses need both manners and social skills. Having good manners means the horse understands who's in charge, respects the space of other horses and humans, and willingly accepts their direction and leadership. A horse with good social skills pays attention to the nuances of communication in a group, knows where he stands in the herd or human-horse hierarchy, and knows which behaviors are appropriate and which ones will not be tolerated.

Spoiled horses may have been allowed to learn bad manners from their humans or they may have been brought up badly by their mothers. Cranky, while leading—but I went back to groundwork again anyway. After about 3 hours of groundwork and about 20 hours of careful, one-step-at-a-time loading practice, he would follow me into the trailer with only a little hesitation and wait for me to tell him when to stand still or back out.

The next problem arose, however, when I secured the tailgate and closed Victor in the trailer. The moment I disappeared from view, he began trembling, pawing, and calling for me. "Abandoned!" he seemed to be crying. "I'm alone and terrified! Come back!"

For a few short trips around the neighborhood, I rode in the trailer with him (illegal in most states and not recommended), and he remained quiet as long as I was patting and talking to him, though he would still break out in a sweat. However, when I left him in the trailer with only a pony for company on our first trip to a neighbor's stable, Victor resumed his frantic calling. Then he began kicking the sides of the trailer.

When I unloaded him just a few minutes later, he twisted around, nipping and kicking at his stomach. His panic was so bad that he'd colicked.

In the past 40 years, I've successfully handled and retrained many difficult loaders and I've never resorted to using sedatives, but Victor was unique. I asked our veterinarian for a supply of acepromazine. I finally decided that this wasn't a failure—it seemed, in fact, to be the only humane thing to do. It was, after all, a major act of faith and trust on Victor's part that he could overcome his terrible fears to follow me into that trailer, but he couldn't face being closed up in that tiny box without some sort of assistance. Just a little bit—about one-third the normal dose—mixed into his feed half an hour before a trip worked to take the edge off his fears, and he was able to load and travel comfortably. Of course, he can't compete in a show with the tranquilizer in his system—but he *can* manage to ride safely by himself in a trailer, which is far more important.

bad-tempered mares tend to have—no surprise here!—pushy, cantankerous, obnoxious foals. A horse who grows up alone, as an orphan or with perhaps only one other horse for companionship, never learns his place or his manners in a herd. He'll test his need for dominance and status on his humans because they have become his herd substitutes.

One of the most effective ways to teach the spoiled horse a little respect is to turn him out in a herd with several wise, experienced, older horses (where the newcomer clearly cannot become dominant), and let the other horses explain the facts of life to him. (This doesn't always work; if the spoiled horse is a big, strong bully, you may not accomplish anything positive.)

Consider the Bitless Bridle

Horses who have had their mouths damaged by harsh bits or rough handling often benefit from the use of a type of bitless bridle. A sidepull or hackamore may help ease their fears about pain in the mouth. There's also the patented Bitless Bridle, developed by researcher Robert Cook, FRCVS, Ph.D.

Cook believes that bits are, by their nature, abusive to the horse; by riding with a bitless bridle, any horse will be more relaxed and happier. A bitless bridle can help reduce or eliminate head tossing, teeth grinding, twisted jaws, bolting, and body tension caused by bit-induced pain. Cook's Bitless Bridle works by putting pressure on several key points: When the reins are tightened, pressure is exerted below the horse's lower jaw, on the bridge of the nose, and at the poll.

Colin McIver

Robert Cook's Bitless Bridle may be a good alternative for very sensitive horses or for those who have suffered bit-related abuse. Pressure points on poll, nose, and under the chin receive signals from the reins.

Nervous or high-strung horses, in particular, seem to do well in Cook's Bitless Bridle, although riders are often concerned they won't have any brakes without a bit. Generally, these concerns appear to be unfounded. I've found that several horses who rushed over jumps, bolted, or jigged under saddle were actually easier to control with the Bitless Bridle than with a bit.

It does seem to be a bit harder to ask for lateral bend with the Bitless Bridle than with a bit. Because the control straps cross under the horse's jaw, putting pressure on one rein puts pressure on both sides of the horse's head. And if the horse's aversion to a bit is caused by dental problems, the Bitless Bridle may not make much of an improvement in performance. However, this bridle may be a very useful alternative for any horse with serious biting issues.

Richard Valcourt

For the spoiled, pushy, disrespectful horse, use a lead chain and a snug-fitting halter. Run the chain through the bottom center ring and up through the left-hand halter ring from inside to outside; wrap it once over the noseband from outside to inside; pass it through the right-hand ring from inside to outside; and clip it to the upper right-hand ring. This configuration should give you an extra measure of control without pulling the halter sideways into your horse's eye. When no pressure is applied to the lead, no chain pressure is applied to the nose. Be sure to release pressure instantly when the horse complies—otherwise, there's no reward for good behavior.

When you handle a spoiled horse, start right at the beginning with groundwork. (See the ground exercises in chapters 6 and 7 and the under-saddle exercises in chapters 11 and 12.) Then . . .

- Use strong, quick, abrupt body movements to control his space. Do lots of lateral work from the ground, and make him wait for his food. Teach him the meaning of *no,* and don't give in.

- Don't let him nip you, grab for grass, tow you anywhere, bump you with a shoulder or hip, or swing around and step on you just because something interesting caught his attention. If he does any of these things, respond with a sharp voice, a jerk on the halter chain, an elbow in the shoulder, or a slap on the muzzle if he nips. The wise, old mare wouldn't tolerate that behavior, and neither should you.

- Use a chain lead every time you handle him, and insist that he respect you by responding promptly every time you ask him to stand, walk beside you, halt, or change direction.

- Spend a lot of time asking the spoiled horse to back on command. Willful, dominant horses do not want to back up because backing is a sign of yielding ground. To back up on command, he must submit to your control.

- Teach him patience by insisting that he stand tied (securely, with a sturdy nylon halter and lead that he cannot break), and leave him tied safely for an hour or two at a time. Be sure everyone else stays safe, and watch for kicking; don't let anyone wander into range of his hind feet.

- Make training sessions short and intense for this horse. He hasn't learned to focus or pay attention, and he probably doesn't have much of an attention span. If you work him too hard for too long before he can handle it, you may create a stubborn, resistant animal who simply shuts down.

- Teach him the meaning of *yes*. Even though you may not like his personality, find every opportunity to give him a reward—but don't use food. Food is too distracting, and it may just teach him that he can grab treats from you whenever he wants them. Teach him to seek nonfood rewards such as wither rubs and your approving voice. Every time he works quietly or waits for your signal before acting, that's a *yes* moment.

For exercises to help solve specific training problems, see chapter 15.

Part II

PROGRESSIVE EXERCISES

6

DISCOVERING TRUST, RESPECT, AND REWARD THROUGH TOUCH

The exercises in this part of the book can help you lay the groundwork for trust, respect, and teamwork with your horse. They're not a complete training program by themselves; rather, they should be used to supplement regular training routines and help you develop a pattern of trust-and-reward behavior and better communication with your horse. The groundwork exercises in chapters 6 through 8 and chapter 14 are suitable for horses of all ages and in all stages of training; the mounted exercises in chapters 9 through 13 are for horses and riders whose basic education has been confirmed but who need a new approach to strengthen their communication skills; and chapter 15 addresses six specific behavior problems.

As you work through these exercises, think about how the 12 principles and 7 key concepts of positive horse training can contribute to every aspect of your work with your horse.

The Purpose of These Exercises

The very basic exercises in this chapter are vital to developing your horse's trust and respect by helping him accept firm, gentle touching everywhere on his body—first with your hands, then with a stick or whip, and finally with something that can feel good but gives him a *little* cause for concern.

Linda Tellington-Jones has developed an extensive system of training and supporting a horse's well-being through touch and massage with her TTeam system. The exercises in this book are not designed to replace or duplicate any of the TTeam exercises; instead, they focus on strengthening your understanding of your horse's *reward spots* and increasing your horse's acceptance of your touch as a reward.

In these exercises, you are asking your horse to stand still, relax, and accept your touch everywhere on his body. You'll also want him to tell you where and how he likes to be touched or not touched and which of your movements bring him pleasure or cause him discomfort. In other words, he's going to tell you how he feels about touch as a reward.

These exercises should help you:

- Learn how and where your horse likes to be touched.
- Find the reward spots on his body.
- Identify the boundaries of his comfort zone.
- Teach your horse that your touch is comforting and rewarding—something to be appreciated rather than feared or merely tolerated.

This is a key part of trust and respect for horses of any age, from month-old foals to mature adults. It's especially useful for a newly acquired horse, as it will tell you volumes about what a horse likes and doesn't like, whether he's willing to trust you, and what he may be concerned about.

What's in the Rewards Toolbox?

- Feel-good pats, scratches, and rubs that provide comfort and release endorphins
- Your positive, approving voice
- Food rewards (optional)

What Do You Need?

Your horse should be wearing a properly fitted nylon or leather halter and a long, thick lead rope. I like an eight-foot-long, fat, cotton lead rope with a heavy brass snap. If your horse has a tendency to pull or barge into you, or otherwise show his disrespect by ignoring a command to stand still, by all means use a nylon rope training halter or a chain leadshank.

A rope halter can be very effective if it's properly fitted so it doesn't slide around and get pulled into the horse's eyes. The thin rope focuses pressure in very precise spots on the bridge of the nose and the poll; many horses who pull their handlers around when wearing a regular flat halter will show considerably more respect in a rope halter.

If you use a chain lead with a snugly fitted flat halter, run it through the left-hand halter ring from outside to inside, then over the noseband just once (so the chain lies mostly across the outside of the noseband), through the offside ring from inside to outside, and up the offside cheek to the throat ring (as shown on page 73). Keep the pressure off the chain as long as the horse is listening to you; apply a quick tug-and-release whenever you need it to remind him to stand still. (And, of course, when he complies, praise and pat!) This should provide just enough incentive to make him understand that he *must* pay attention to you.

You can do these exercises anywhere that gives you enough room to move around your horse: in a 12-foot-square stall, a pasture, a round pen, or an arena. Be sure you won't be crowded against a wall or corner, and if your horse is young or easily distracted, make sure there are no other horses around to divert his attention. You want your horse to focus entirely on you so that you can pay close attention to him as well.

Step One

Begin on the horse's left side, holding the lead rope in your left hand and using your right hand (no gloves, please!) to rub all over his body. Begin in the middle of his neck and move across his shoulders and over his back and rump. Then return to the front and go over his chest, shoulders, ribcage, abdomen, and lower hindquarters. Last, tackle the most sensitive areas: face, legs, and inside the flanks and gaskins.

If your horse offers to lift a foot when you touch a leg, just remove your hand, let him put the foot down, and go back to rubbing and stroking until he stands on all fours. Likewise, if he moves sideways when you touch his ribcage, he may think you want him to move away from pressure. Again, ease off, ask him to stand, then go back to the same spot, perhaps with a lighter touch.

Use your whole hand and fingertips in a firm but gentle circular motion, and vary the pressure to see what your horse likes. Don't pat or slap—keep the contact as you move from place to place. Look for *yes* signals: lowered head, relaxed ears, easy breathing, chewing. When you get strong yes signals, spend a little more time in that spot and vary the touch so you're stroking more firmly or scratching more vigorously.

Spend at least half an hour just exploring your horse's body. And be careful: When you reach an itchy spot, your horse may turn and offer to scratch *your* back, too, so be careful you're not where he can reach you with his teeth to perform vigorous reciprocal scratching.

When you reach a spot that causes him to fidget, shake his head, flatten his ears, or give you other *no* signals, back off. You've stepped outside his comfort zone. Don't force it—he's giving you important information about what he doesn't like. Remind him firmly to stand still, return to a known pleasure spot, and then try varying your touch in the more sensitive area—go a little firmer or a little softer. In other words, push the edges of the comfort zone a little. Don't tickle your horse, however, or touch so lightly that the muscles in his skin try to shake you off like an annoying fly. Think of how another horse would rub or nuzzle him in affection, and try to duplicate that touch.

Be quietly persistent. Your goal is to have him relax, trust, and accept the touch of your hand everywhere on his body.

Step Two

After you've touched every inch of his body with reassuring rubs, you should have a pretty good idea of how he likes to be touched and where. Now you can focus on three specific reward spots—the face, the withers, and just above the tail. These are key endorphin producers, and you'll be able to use these areas frequently in training.

Start with the withers, the universal buddy-grooming spot. Rub or scratch firmly on the crest of your horse's neck, just in front of the withers. Concentrate on the spot closest to where your hands are when you're riding, and give him a few minutes of circular rubbing or scratching.

Then move to his rump, and rub the spot just above his tail. This is the spot a mare can reach to nuzzle her foal while he's nursing, and it's very important for bonding.

Finally, move to your horse's head and rub his forehead between the eyes. Most horses also seem to be soothed by having a hand run down over the eyes. Many also like to have their ears gently stroked, and others love to have the itchy spot under their chin scratched. Begin with the forehead, but locate the other pleasure spots on your horse's face as well.

Why is it important for you to cultivate these three reward spots? Because you need to have a touch reward in your toolbox whenever possible. You can reach the forehead or withers while leading or ponying; the rump while driving, ground driving, or working on your horse's hind legs; and the withers while riding.

Step Three

After you've found your horse's key touch-reward spots, you can move on to touch with a stick or whip.

Your horse should not fear a whip. A whip is an important signaling device, an extension of your arm. If your horse won't accept the quiet use of a whip or stick, you're handicapped because you can't use an important tool for communication. A sharply applied whip may occasionally be necessary to correct a severe and dangerous disobedience, but it should *never* be used as an instrument of anger or pain.

Introduce your horse to a riding crop, dressage whip, or three-foot stick by offering it to him to smell and examine. Then place it quietly against his neck and begin stroking in long, firm movements. Don't ruffle his hair; stroke head-to-tail and downward, following the direction of hair growth. Move a little more slowly than you did when you were using your hand. Each movement of the stick is exaggerated at the tip, so be careful not to make quick, unpredictable movements.

As long as your horse is showing yes signals, continue moving the stick over his whole body, beginning with the larger, less-sensitive parts of his body and then moving on to his legs, abdomen, and head. Don't force him to accept this; just continue moving the stick over the parts of the body that he's comfortable with, retreat when he shows discomfort, and return to the trouble spots later.

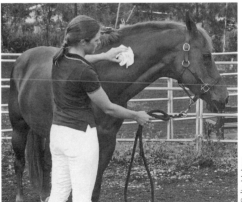

Key endorphin-releasing spots are the forehead, the withers, and just above the tail. Teach your horse to look forward to touches and rubs in these three spots, and be sure to add your praising voice so he knows that both are indicators of your approval. Five-year-old Taser is giving very clear yes signals to a forehead rub: lowered head, relaxed ears, soft eyes.

Many horses do not like the sound or feeling of crinkly paper but will learn to accept it if it comes with your approval voice and rubs in their favorite spots. Coosa Lani has turned away, perhaps in mild avoidance, but is willing to stand quietly and tolerate the exercise. Be careful not to annoy your horse's ticklish spots (flanks, belly, between the hind legs) by touching too lightly with the paper. Use the two-handed approach to offer comforting reward touches along with the touch of the paper.

As Lisa moves her dressage whip quietly but firmly over Taser's body, she keeps an eye on the mare's responses. The position of Taser's ears, eyes, and head show that she's slightly anxious about the whip but is still willing to stand still and pay attention. This activity is within her comfort zone; she may not like it, but she accepts it. Lisa adds her approval voice and an occasional forehead rub to reduce anxiety and let Taser know she's responding correctly by standing quietly.

Every few minutes, *reward*! Being touched with a stick isn't much of a reward, but being rubbed in one of his favorites spots by your hand *is* a reward. Use your other hand to rub or scratch his withers, and praise with your best, quietest, most soothing good-boy voice.

Step Four

After your horse is comfortable with all-over touch from your hands and the whip and you've learned where his best reward spots are, repeat the touching exercises with different items. First, introduce a soft towel, then a piece of wadded up newspaper that makes a little rustling sound, and then a piece of noisy, crinkling cellophane.

Most horses are quite happy to accept a soft towel, as the feel won't be too much different from that of your hand and there's virtually no noise involved. However, if the towel is large, bright white, and moves around a lot, it may be a bit more challenging. Pay attention to the signals he's giving you, and move back and forth across the lines of his comfort zone until he relaxes.

Try rubbing him with the wadded up newspaper, which will be a little scratchy and will make noises as you touch him with it. A good method here is to use two hands: one to hold the newspaper and the other right next to it to apply familiar rubs and scratches in the reward spots.

Once he accepts the newspaper, introduce other harmless but potentially anxiety-causing items, such as rustling cellophane or a child's squeaky toy. Simulate the pleasurable hand rubbing you performed in step one, but allow your horse to also hear the funny noises and feel the strange texture.

If your horse simply refuses to accept the presence or touch of a strange object, food rewards can be helpful. Offer a carrot several times while crinkling the cellophane or squeaking the toy, and soon your horse will associate only good things with the new sounds. If the carrot sits in the cellophane and the rustling sound happens as a natural result of unwrapping the reward, most horses will quickly appreciate that good things can arrive with the cellophane. (One friend has made a habit of feeding her horses peppermints as treats; the sound of cellophane being unwrapped brings them running.)

In case you're wondering why you should ask your horse to be touched with cellophane, this is a simple example of low-threat combat training: You create simulated dangers, push the edges of your horse's comfort zone, ask him to accept your guidance and offer his trust, and then provide rewards for his obedience. Combat training is explained in depth in chapter 14.

7

DEVELOPING THE HABITS OF PLEASE AND THANK YOU

The Purpose of These Exercises

The goal of this series of ground exercises is to gain complete control of both ends of the horse from the ground. You should end up with a horse who walks, trots, turns, backs up, and stands quietly at your shoulder while on a slack lead rope. He will also step sideways and perform a simple turn on the forehand— all with minimal direction from you.

This series of exercises provides many benefits. It can help you:

- Develop patterns of obedience and control with any horse, from weanlings to old campaigners who need a little brush-up in manners.

- Learn better timing and communication in your requests and rewards.

- Improve your horse's balance, agility, and engagement of the hindquarters.

- Prepare a young horse to begin work under saddle by introducing lateral movements and reinbacks.

- Identify crookedness and strengthen your horse's weaker or less-flexible side.

What's in the Rewards Toolbox?

- Release of pressure
- Feel-good pats, scratches, and rubs
- Your positive, approving voice
- Rest and relaxation

What Do You Need?

Your horse should have a halter and lead rope. If your horse tends to barge forward or haul you around, outfit him with a rope training halter or supplement his flat halter with a chain lead (as shown on page 73).

You can also tack up with a bridle and saddle and perform any or all of the same exercises just before riding. Lateral work on the ground is especially valuable as preparation for lateral work under saddle.

If your horse is dull to the leg when you ride or does not move forward promptly when you ask him to trot on the lead and you're using these exercises to sharpen up his responses or introduce lateral work, you'll also need a whip or flexible stick about 40 inches long.

Step One

First, confirm your basic leading skills. Stand on the left by your horse's head in basic leading position, with your right hand on the lead about six inches away from the halter and your rope gathered in your left hand. If you feel you'll need to carry the whip to reinforce "forward," also put that in your left hand with the lash end pointing back behind you.

Look straight ahead and give your horse an alert signal—a small movement that will say, "Attention, please." Some trainers like to lean their upper body forward slightly, ready to take the first step. I like to slightly raise my leading hand (the one that's closest to the halter) about an inch and straighten my stance a little taller *without* putting any pressure on the halter. Many trainers who show in breed classes will raise their hand considerably higher. Your horse won't know what the alert signal means the first few times you use it, but he'll quickly come to look for it if you use it consistently.

A second after you've given your alert signal, say, "walk" and step briskly forward. The horse should move with you, with his head even with your shoulder. Don't put any pressure on the lead as long as he stays at your shoulder, where he belongs.

If your horse doesn't follow immediately when you step forward, give a quick, sharp tug on the halter, release just as quickly, repeat the command "walk," and move right out again. If he's *really* ignoring you and just plants his feet or reluctantly crawls after you, quickly move back to his shoulder, bring your left hand (holding the whip) around behind your body, and (*without looking back*) tap him sharply on the hindquarters. It's important to keep looking where you want to go; don't twist around and confuse your horse about which direction he's supposed to move. Tap once sharply and immediately move forward as you repeat the command "walk." Be prepared for him to startle forward or sideways in response to the whip. Walk about 10 feet, then ask him to stop with a verbal "whoa" and light pressure on the halter, if needed, and offer praise.

What if your horse barges ahead of you, treading on your feet and hauling you along with him? Give a sharp tug-and-release on your lead and *immediately* change directions, snapping him around to the left. If necessary, set your right elbow sharply into the horse's neck just in front of the shoulder for leverage. Say "walk" again and head off in the new direction. The moment he barges ahead, tug sharply, pivot, and snap him around again. The message you're conveying is that *you* control his space and direction, and if he's not going to acknowledge that, you're going to make him uncomfortable by forcing him to adjust his momentum and work harder to recover his balance.

Whether your horse responds promptly or not, your timing is critical. You've given him a whole set of communication aids to reinforce your simple command. By providing him with several strong cues—visual (moving forward), tactile (pressure on the halter), verbal ("walk")—you've made it absolutely clear what you want, and you're not springing anything on him because you've added that small *please* at the beginning.

Step Two

Once you've confirmed that your horse will move smartly forward at the walk without barging or lagging behind, follow the same procedure to develop a good trot in hand. Give your alert signal (*please*), make your request, correct if necessary, ask again, and reward (*thank you*) with praise, rest, and release of pressure.

Then begin varying the speed at the walk and trot. Whether you move at a slow, sauntering walk, a brisk march, a quiet jog, or a very forward trot, your horse should keep pace and keep his head at your shoulder. Make your changes in speed gradual at first so that your horse has time to make the necessary adjustments to his balance. When you do make abrupt changes in speed, give clear, alert signals to prepare him.

Add gentle turns in both directions, then gradually tighten the turns. To give an alert signal for a turn, raise your hand slightly as you look and then turn your body in the direction you plan to go. Your goal is to produce turns and changes in direction with no contact on the halter. If your horse pays attention and keeps his head near your shoulder, provide plenty of praise. If he's not paying attention, give that sharp tug-and-release or add a tap of the whip for emphasis. Your body language should provide enough of a command for him to change speed within the walk or trot, but some people like to add the verbal commands "walk *on*" or "trot *on*" as they speed up, or "easy" as they slow down. Whatever you use, be clear and consistent!

After you feel he's confirmed in good leading manners with you on his left, switch sides and repeat everything from the right. You may both feel clumsy at this, especially if you've led horses only from the left side for a few decades, but it's imperative that you work equally from both sides in *all* your training. The

---

Head to Shoulder or Shoulder to Shoulder?

Some trainers like a horse to walk slightly ahead of them with the horse's shoulder aligned with the handler's shoulder. This preference is seen in some of the breed shows and in the traditions of the European warmblood inspections, in which the horses are encouraged to trot slightly ahead of the handlers to better display the head, neck, and shoulders. When the judges are viewing the horse from the offside, the handler seems to disappear behind the horse, and the horse can demonstrate free, forward, unconstrained movement.

Unfortunately, this leading position can put the handler uncomfortably close to the horse's front feet, and horses taught to lead in this manner often seem to be making all the decisions about where and how fast to move.

For safety and control, especially when working with small children or green horses, I've always preferred the horse's head to be aligned with my shoulder or never more than a few inches in front. If you are competing in shows where the horse-ahead position is the norm, you can ask your horse to learn *both* methods of leading. To ask him to move out ahead of you, carry your whip behind your body and gesture with it to signal your horse to move forward ahead of you when required. Develop a set of signals (hand gestures, voice, a cluck) to ask for the big, brilliant movement that you'll want to display to the judges. Then go back to the head-at-your-shoulder position after you've left the show ring.

---

debate will always rage about whether horses are born crooked, but one thing is certain: If you always handle your horse from the left, you will create a crooked horse. To be an effective trainer, you need to be equally comfortable working on the right or the left, whether longeing, leading, or mounting.

Step Three

Now that your horse is paying close attention to you as you walk forward, ask for a halt by walking straight toward a fence or other barrier, then raising your leading hand slightly, stopping your forward motion, and saying, "whoa." Add a backward tug-and-release on the halter if necessary. After the horse halts, let him rest for a moment. Don't ask for a perfectly square halt, just a quiet and relatively balanced one. Praise! Being allowed to rest is a reward, but your horse also needs to know he has your approval whenever he does something correctly.

He should stop when you stop, since you've already been working on the *stay with me when I slow down* exercise in step two. Reward a prompt, quiet halt. If he halts and then creeps forward, correct him with a quick, backward tug-and-release on the halter and repeat your "whoa." If he leans forward and threatens to walk over you, snap him around in a sharp turn and repeat your request for a halt, then reward immediately so the connection between response and reward is a little stronger.

As soon as he's responding reliably to the request for a halt, begin asking him to stand still for two or three minutes at a time as you move around him. Each time he starts to move away or his attention seems to wander, ask again for a halt, reinforce the command with a tug on the halter as needed, and then reward him. Remember to use the top-of-tail reward spot as you move behind him. Your horse should stand quietly and attentively until you give him a clear signal to move off.

Think of how you can reinforce this training and put these practical skills to work. Ask for a halt before leading your horse through a barn doorway or a gate so that your horse waits and allows you to step through without crowding. Reinforce your halt command every time you mount, and keep your horse standing quietly as you adjust stirrups or girth. Ask him to halt and stand for the farrier or veterinarian.

From the halt, you can now ask for a few steps backward. Turn and face your horse, standing in front (but also allowing him a place to go other than straight over the top of you if he resists and shoots forward). Push straight back on the lead rope so he feels halter pressure on the bridge of his nose, say "back," and take a step toward him. Release the halter pressure, and praise him the moment he steps backward. Repeat, asking for two or three steps backward.

Don't rush him; you want careful, measured, balanced steps backward with no resistance or awkwardness. Horses don't like to back up—it's a strong sign of submission. Reward him for each attempt, and don't ask for too much too soon. If he flings his head up or lurches to the side, let him settle and then ask again for just one good step.

Once you've got your horse backing up willingly for half a dozen steps or more, introduce a pair of parallel ground poles placed six to eight feet apart and practice backing him through the poles. As he becomes more adept at this exercise, you can reduce the spacing between the poles so he finds it more challenging to go straight back. When he steps onto or over a pole, lead him forward a few steps to straighten him out and ask him to back again.

Don't ever punish your horse for being awkward or hitting a pole! Horses don't like to step onto or bump against things with their feet—it threatens their ability to get away from danger—so additional punishment will simply make him more resistant to complying with your request to step backward. Just be patient and move back to a slightly easier exercise if he's having trouble.

Step Four

Now you can introduce lateral work with a quarter-turn on the forehand. Halt your horse directly in front of and about two feet away from a fence or other barrier. The barrier will help your horse understand the logic of moving sideways to move forward.

Stand on his left side, holding the lead rope in your left hand. Place the palm and heel of your hand against his barrel about where your lower leg would lie if you were riding. Quietly placing your hand is the alert signal; it mimics the presence of your neutral leg position when you're riding. With your left hand,

Rachel is in basic leading position, ready to touch Willa on the hindquarters with the whip if the mare lags behind. Perhaps because of the whip, Willa is determined not to be left behind, and the mare's head has moved slightly ahead of Rachel's shoulder, but she is relaxed and attentive to her handler.

Rachel has asked Willa to pause before going through a narrow gateway—a vital component of both good manners and safety. Willa has halted calmly, and Rachel has rewarded her with verbal praise and a release of pressure on the halter.

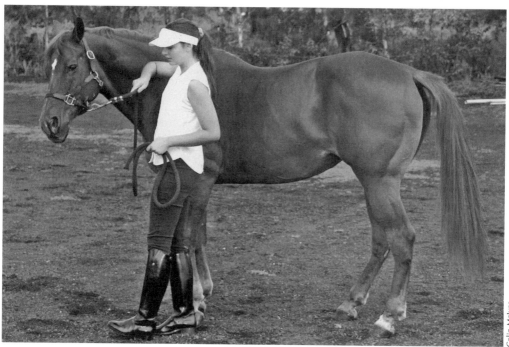

Coosa Lani has pulled ahead of her handler, so Emily has stopped abruptly, set her elbow into the mare's neck just ahead of the shoulder, and is about to spin sharply around and head in the opposite direction. This is an effective method of dealing with a horse who tries to take over the leadership position. Once Coosa Lani accepts Emily's guidance, the mare will be rewarded with comfort, balance, and praise from her human leader.

Richard Valcourt

Emily has begun asking Coosa Lani to step backward by signaling with request-response-release pressure on the halter. She's also placed her hand on the mare's barrel in preparation for asking the horse's hips to move sideways when she reaches the corner. In a second, Emily's left hand will slide a few inches lower to mimic the pressure of a rider's leg, and she'll draw the horse's head a little toward her to allow the hindquarters to move away. Coosa Lani is responding nicely, with lowered head . . .

. . . and smooth hips-sideways steps to maneuver around the corner.

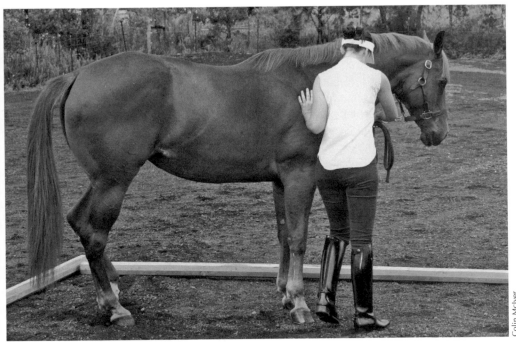

Colin McIver

To move her horse's forehand sideways, Emily places her hand on Coosa Lani's shoulder, asks the mare to step a little backward to shift weight onto her hindquarters, and directs her shoulders away as they maneuver in the box.

turn his head a little toward you as you press and release with the heel of your hand on his barrel. Your horse should take a step or two to the right with his hindquarters. Repeat the request to step over until he has completed a quarter-turn and his body is parallel to the fence. Then praise him and walk forward.

Practice a few more times on the same side, then switch sides and work on turns away from pressure on his right side. If he doesn't respond to pressure from the heel and palm of your hand, create a sharper pressure by making a fist and pushing with a knuckle or two. If *that* doesn't work, use the butt end of your whip to poke into his side. Be patient, and be ready to release and reward the very *instant* he responds correctly. You must also be prepared to correct him with a sharp tug, a slap, and a *no* if he thinks that waving a hind foot or kicking will get rid of the annoyance in his ribs.

A note of caution: Some horses will begin to anticipate and will start stepping sideways as soon as you merely gesture toward their ribs. Overworking your horse in this exercise may cause him to think he's supposed to shift sideways every time you ask for a halt. Confirm the halt before you ask for any lateral movement, and don't overdo it!

Step Five

The last step is to gain lateral control of the shoulders. This turn-on-the-haunches exercise, combined with backing exercises, can help your horse learn to lighten and mobilize his front end—a major goal in riding no matter what the discipline. It's also a baby-steps introduction to the concept of turning from outside rein pressure, useful for teaching neckreining in western riding and bending from the outside aids in dressage.

Begin at a halt. Stand in front of your horse's left shoulder, facing him, with the lead rope in your left hand. Ask him to back a few steps to help him shift his weight toward the rear and then place your right hand on the front of his shoulder blade about midway between the withers and the point of the shoulder. Push against his shoulder while pushing his head away a little with your left hand. He should yield to the pressure, stepping sideways with his front feet and pivoting on his hind feet. If he's confused or seems to be stuck, try placing your left hand on his shoulder and your right hand farther back on his barrel, in the same position you used for the turn on the forehand. The hand on his barrel should keep his hindquarters from moving toward you while the hand on his shoulder helps the shoulders move away.

Timing is critical here: You want to ask the shoulders to move while his weight is still back on his hindquarters, so ask the shoulders to move at the moment he's finished a step backward.

Step Six

Now you can put it all together to execute a few classic trail-class maneuvers from the ground.

Fine-tune your backing skills. Set up L-shaped or angled back-up poles, and ask your horse to back quietly through them, asking him to pause and shift his hindquarters or shoulders over as needed to negotiate the turns.

Create turns inside a square. Use four 10-foot ground poles (or 12-foot poles, if your horse is very large) to create a square. Ask your horse to step into the square, complete a 360-degree turn, and walk out. Perform the turns using a turn on the forehand, a turn on the haunches, or a combination of both. At every step, ask for calm, steady responses, not speed—and reward, reward, reward!

8

ESSENTIAL WARM-UP STRETCHES FOR YOUR HORSE

The Purpose of These Exercises

In these preride exercises, you'll be asking your horse to stand still and relax, yield to lateral and longitudinal rein pressure, allow his neck muscles and forelegs to be stretched and massaged, and give you feedback so you'll be able to recognize his signs of acceptance, trust, and pleasure.

Doing these exercises will help your horse better understand how to:

- Yield to rein pressure from either side.

- Soften his jaw when you pick up the contact.

- Stretch his topline so he'll be able to use his back and hindquarters more effectively.

You'll also demonstrate to the horse that you can help him feel more comfortable by stretching key muscles before working. (Have you ever ridden a horse who truly looked forward to training sessions in the arena? Enjoyable, wasn't it? This may help your horse actually look forward to work sessions.)

Equally important, this series of exercises should help you think about how you reward your horse by releasing pressure and helping him restore his balance.

These exercises are appropriate for every horse, young or old, but they especially benefit horses with strong, thick, or heavily muscled necks and those who are stiff in the neck or shoulders at the beginning of work sessions. I developed this routine for the Quarter Horse mare shown in the photos, who often had a stiff, grouchy, and uncooperative attitude at the beginning of each training session. I've since used it with very good results on many other horses.

These exercises put horses in a more relaxed, willing frame of mind because they're feeling more supple and comfortable right at the *beginning* of the training session—and because the exercises help trainers remember to provide rewards right from the beginning.

Once you've established a rhythm for this series of exercises, they should take no more than five minutes at the beginning of each work session.

Note that the first two flexion exercises are beneficial for heavyset horses but aren't always helpful for those with long, thin, undermuscled necks. You will want your horse to soften his jaw and yield to your hand, not curl up into a little ball. If his response is to bring his head inside the vertical and tuck his chin on his chest to avoid all rein pressure, stop this exercise and move on.

What's in the Rewards Toolbox?

- Pleasurable touching and massage
- Release of pressure
- Reward-spot scratches and rubs on the withers and forehead
- A greater range of comfortable motion and more balance under saddle
- As always, your voice of approval

What Do You Need?

Have your horse tacked up and ready to work in a snaffle bridle, longeing cavesson, or bitless bridle. If you are longeing, leave off the longe line and don't fasten the sidereins to the surcingle. If you are driving, you can have your horse harnessed but not hitched. Don't tighten the girth or surcingle more than necessary to keep everything in place. Many horses become distressed and resistant if the girth is overtightened or tightened too quickly, and this exercise will help them become more comfortable with the saddling, girthing, and preride process.

To begin, lead your horse into the center of your arena, away from distractions, obstacles, and other horses. Check to be sure the girth is only snug enough to keep the saddle or surcingle from slipping.

Step One

The first part of this exercise asks for softening of the jaw and longitudinal (lengthwise) flexion.

While standing by your horse's left shoulder and facing forward, take up the reins evenly, just in front of the horse's withers and a little forward of where your hands would be if you were riding. Keeping steady contact on the right rein, lift your left hand about three inches and vibrate the rein slightly with what some trainers call a *palsied* or *trembling* hand. When your horse drops his head and softens his jaw with a relaxed chewing motion, *immediately release* both reins, reward him with pats or rubs in the nearest reward spot, and give your approval voice.

Do this three or four times, then move to his right shoulder and repeat from the offside, keeping steady contact on the left rein and asking for the flexion with the raised right rein.

If he doesn't drop his head and soften his jaw (or if he twists away, pulls against your hand, or raises his head), keep the contact, stay with him, and ask again with a vibrating hand. Do not punish or try to correct him. If he backs up, reposition him so his tail is close to a fence corner or other barrier and ask again. Be patient. After perhaps three or four tries, he should figure it out through trial and error. And be sure to release and reward promptly, even if the drop-and-yield movement is a very small one. Reward every step of the process, not just the perfect response. And wait for half a minute before asking again; many horses need time to process the information before it sinks in.

Step Two

Next, ask your horse to flex laterally (side to side). Stand at his left shoulder and take up only the left rein, just in front of and a little below the horse's withers. Exert quiet, vibrating contact on the rein until he turns his head to the left. Immediately release and reward with wither rubs and your approval voice. Repeat this two or three times on the left, then move to the offside and repeat with the right rein. If your horse seems a little more stiff or reluctant on one side, work a little more on that side. It's okay if he drops his head a little as he yields to each side, but he shouldn't twist or cock his head unevenly. Look for even flexion to each side, with both ears remaining at the same height.

If he doesn't flex to either side or if he raises his head, keep the contact, stay with him, and ask again. Don't punish or escalate your demands, just maintain steady contact with a little vibration.

After you've done this a few times, you can ask him to hold the lateral flexion just a second or two longer each time. Release and reward promptly, but don't drop the rein entirely. Release it just an inch or two, so your horse feels contact again when he starts to swing his head around to the front. Ask for a return to the flexed position, then release completely and reward. Your goal in this is to help him eventually learn to carry himself in softness and flexion, not have you hold him there with a heavy hand.

Step Three

Now that you've stretched the horse's neck a bit, give it a good massage. Find the deep muscles just in front of the shoulder blade (see the photo on page 97), make a fist, and knead with your knuckles for about 30 seconds on each side. See if you can find muscles that feel knotted—stress and muscle spasms can make these muscles uncomfortably tight. Some horses don't want much pressure at first, so you'll have to find out what your horse will accept and go easy on him. However, many horses learn to love a deep neck massage and will lean right into it.

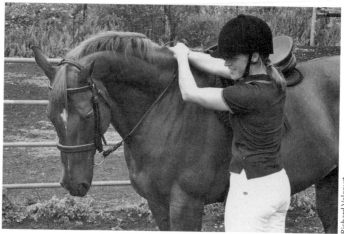

Richard Valcourt

Meredith has asked Coosa Lani to soften her jaw and flex longitudinally by fixing the right rein while lifting and vibrating the left rein. The right rein should be a little shorter to avoid flexion to the side, but this photo shows a nicely compliant mare with a relaxed jaw and soft eye.

Colin McIver

This sideways flexion demonstrates the mare's willingness to soften and yield her powerful neck. She gives to the vibrating rein without twisting her head or opening her mouth. One second later, Meredith will drop the rein and give rewards of relaxation, release of pressure, and an approving voice.

Coosa Lani appreciates the neck-muscle massage Meredith is giving her. She's attentive but very relaxed—a happy horse who's already receiving pleasurable rewards, even before her rider gets on.

As you stretch your horse's front legs, be sure to lift with your legs, not just your back. This exercise stretches the horse's shoulder muscles and removes any wrinkled skin under the girth.

After you've mounted and allowed your horse to stretch into a relaxed walk, halt and ask for the same neck-flexion exercises that you practiced on the ground. In this photo, Coosa Lani is giving a rather extreme stretch, but she's showing no signs of tension, and the right rein isn't quite as taut as it appears—see how soft Meredith's hands look and how well she has maintained the straight line from her elbow to the bit. She has also kept her legs right where they belong, with her right leg resting passively on the girth and her left leg firmly against Coosa Lani's left ribcage to ensure that the mare doesn't swing her haunches to the left.

Step Four

You should now be able to tighten your girth a notch or two without any complaints from your horse. Do it gently, and don't overtighten. Then pick up one of your horse's front legs and stretch it straight forward as far as he will allow, hold it for three seconds, and put it down. Repeat with the other front leg. This stretches the shoulder muscles and also pulls loose skin out from under the girth so your horse will feel more comfortable about moving forward.

Step Five

Mount up, warm up for a few minutes in a relaxed walk, then halt and ask for the same neck stretches as you asked for from the ground (steps one and two). If your horse shifts sideways or seems to think the request for side-to-side flexion is a request for forward motion and a turn, position him in front of a fence or wall to block his motion in that direction and ask again for the flexion. Add a little outside leg to help hold his hindquarters in place (right leg if you're flexing left, left leg if you're flexing right), or ask a friend to stay by his head to encourage him to stand still.

Be careful not to overdo these stretch exercises, especially with a young horse, as it can be easy for the horse to confuse the signals for correct bending and lateral movements at other stages of training. Use these exercises only as part of your warm-up, and be sure to reward frequently so the beginning of each ride is pleasant to the horse.

9

FINDING YOUR BALANCE IN THE SADDLE, I

The Purpose of These Exercises

These exercises will help you find or improve your balance in the saddle. An unbalanced horse is an uncomfortable horse seeking to become comfortable. But you can't help your horse balance if you can't keep yourself balanced and secure. If a horse can't trust his rider to help him establish balance and restore comfort and security, he'll seek his own solutions and ignore the rider.

Sensitive horses have very little tolerance for unbalanced riders, and they won't respect a rider who bounces at the trot (because she can't follow the horse's rhythm) or one whose hands leap up and down in a posting trot (because her elbows are locked and she's using her hands for balance).

By improving your balance in the saddle, you'll improve your status as a confident, competent, predictable guide—someone who's worthy of the leadership position. As your balance improves, you'll be better able to use your natural aids (seat, legs, and hands) independently, and your horse will be better able to understand your clear, direct, intentional signals.

If you jump, you may already be working in two-point position during riding sessions. If so, you can use these exercises as a checklist to make sure your balance is as secure as you think it is.

What's in the Rewards Toolbox?

Because this is an exercise to improve your balance, not your horse's responsiveness, you'll make only very simple demands and therefore use simple rewards. You'll try to sit lightly, not disrupt the horse's balance, and make position changes gently so your mount can stay relaxed and comfortable. Rewards for the horse include:

- Lightening of the rider's leg after the correct (go forward) response
- Frequent rest breaks

- Your positive, approving voice
- Appreciative pats and withers rubs

What Do You Need?

You need to put yourself on a trustworthy horse who will travel steadily at a walk and trot in a large circle with no rein contact. If you're working in a round pen that is 45 to 60 feet in diameter and your horse can be trusted to follow the perimeter and maintain a steady rhythm, you can work alone. Otherwise you'll need a longe line, a horse who is trained to longe, and a friend to direct the horse on the longe line. Having an extra person on the ground to tell you if everything looks right can also be helpful.

Step One

Tack up your horse as usual, but tie an extra knot in the reins so you can drop the reins on his neck and ride hands-free. If you're using a longe line, attach it to the inside ring of the snaffle bit or a halter under the bridle. Don't attach the line to any part of a shank (curb) bit.

In this exercise, you'll be working mostly in two-point or jumping position. (This actually has very little to do with jumping. Whether you are already jumping four-foot fences, you intend to learn to jump in the future, or you never plan to jump at all—this is a back-to-basics exercise that develops critical skills for all ages, all levels, and all riding disciplines.)

Begin at a standstill. Drop your knotted reins on your horse's neck or loop them over the saddle horn; where you place them isn't important, as long as the reins don't fall under your horse's feet or put uneven pressure on his mouth, and you can still pick them up if you need them. Be sure your stirrups are the right length: With your feet out of the stirrups and your legs stretched long, the stirrup tread should be even with your ankles. You'll want the stirrups short enough to raise your seat an inch or two out of the saddle while still maintaining an angle in the hips, knees, and ankles.

Now close your (empty) hands in loose fists and place your knuckles lightly against the crest of your horse's neck, three to four inches ahead of the saddle. Keep your feet directly under your body, lift your seat out of the saddle, fold a little forward at the hip, and allow your weight to sink into your heels. Keep your shoulders square and don't round your back. Be sure you've got the same amount of weight in each stirrup and look up! This is your basic two-point position, so-called because your two legs are your two points of contact for balance and communication with your horse.

Spend a couple of minutes finding your balance in two-point position at a standstill. Use two fingers to hold onto the mane for support at first if you need to. The key is to keep your feet under you because if your feet and lower legs slide back, you'll tip forward and end up on your horse's neck. If your feet swing forward, you'll flop back in the saddle. Either way, you're going to annoy your horse and upset his balance, so stay over your feet! If you're in a western saddle or a very deep dressage saddle, you may have to shorten your stirrups a little to bring your seat out of the saddle while still keeping the bend in your knees. Don't perch on the pommel, hold the horn, or lean on the swell—that's cheating, and it won't help you improve your balance.

Once you're comfortable at a standstill, ask your horse to first walk and then trot in the round pen or on the longe line while you balance in two-point position. Your goal is to remain in a comfortable, balanced two-point position for several minutes at a trot in each direction, without holding the mane or leaning on your horse's neck. You should also be able to manage gait transitions (walk-trot and walk-halt) without touching the reins; simply close your lower legs and squeeze for upward transitions, or lighten the contact in your lower legs and bring your shoulders back a bit for downward transitions. Discover how much influence you can have on your horse's speed, rhythm, and gait using just your position, weight, and leg aids. (Not all horses respond the same way when they're put into lesson mode. Veteran lesson horses may ignore much of what goes on in the saddle during these exercises and may not pay much attention to your attempts to send them signals while in two-point position. Green horses, on the other hand, may be very sensitive and may respond either hesitantly or rather abruptly to your shifts in balance and the nonexistent rein contact.)

Colin McIver

Balance over your feet, with your weight in your heels and your back straight. Fold at the hip; don't collapse your back. Maintain a straight line from your elbows along your forearms and wrists toward the bit.

Colin McIver

Once you're comfortable at the walk, try the same exercise at a trot and then over simple cavaletti. Although this exercise seems simple, many non–hunt seat riders find it a new experience. Lisa, a dressage rider, found that her legs became stronger after she began jumping. Here, she practices moving her hands from a neutral at-the-withers position . . .

Colin McIver

. . . to a crest release without shifting her balance or making any big moves that would distract Taser or upset her balance. If your balance is steady and solid in two-point position, try shifting from sitting trot to posting trot to two-point position and back to sitting trot without collapsing, changing the position of your legs, or disrupting your horse's balance and rhythm. Jan Dawson, in her book *Teaching Safe Horsemanship,* recommends this exercise for all riders in all disciplines as a way to strengthen balance and security in the saddle.

Richard Valcourt

Whatever your discipline, the basics are the same: Center your balance over your feet, and develop the independent use of your hands, legs, and weight. Riding slightly more upright in her western endurance saddle than she would in her jumping saddle, Lori easily maintains her no-hands balance at the trot.

Step Two

After you can comfortably manage a two-point position at a walk and a trot without holding on, begin experimenting with arm and hand positions. Hold your arms out horizontally at shoulder height, or place your hands on your hips while holding your two-point position. You'll find it's even harder to place your arms in different positions, but try it: Hold one arm straight out in front of you and the other to the side, or place one hand on your hip and stretch the other arm straight up. Make all your movements and changes smooth and steady. Don't frighten your horse or disrupt his rhythm or your own balance.

Your goal is to stay centered over your saddle with your weight evenly distributed in both stirrups, regardless of where your hands and arms go. You're training yourself to create independent aids so that your seat, legs, and hands can work either separately or together, as needed.

Take frequent breaks, and reward your horse often with your positive voice and pats for putting up with what is for him a fairly boring exercise.

Step Three

Now it's time to master (or confirm) the release of hands and arms. From your two-point position at the trot, practice releasing your hands forward. Begin with the basic no-reins hand position and then, at a predetermined spot on your circle (or when your helper calls "release!"), push your hands an inch or two forward and *downward*, toward your horse's mouth. Hold the release position for three or four steps, then quietly return to the basic hand position.

If you like, you can practice this over a ground pole or a series of ground poles (cavaletti). Be sure to release one step before the first rail and hold the release position until the horse's hind feet have cleared the last rail.

Note: Only your hands and arms should move into the release. Don't drop your shoulders; lean or lie on the horse's neck; or make any movements with your torso, hips, or legs. (In jumping, you would also fold at the hips as you release with your hands, but that's not the point with this exercise.)

Step Four

This is a good exercise for helping you develop steady contact on the reins. Try shortening and lengthening the reins while keeping the horseshoes at exactly the same height.

Now you can dismount and give your horse a break. This exercise was first developed to teach expert rein handling to carriage drivers.

Connect a pair of reins to a couple of old horseshoes and rig the reins so they slide freely through a pair of hooks or pad eyes on a fence or wall at about the height of your waist. Hold the reins as if you were mounted, and practice shortening and lengthening your reins an inch or half an inch at a time while keeping both horseshoes at exactly the same height. This sounds easy, but it's actually quite difficult to adjust the length while keeping even tension on both reins.

Step Five

Now you can leave the longe line or round pen, get back on your horse, go into your large arena, and take up the reins. Pick up the trot, go into two-point position, and practice each of the following:

- Shorten and lengthen your reins an inch or half an inch at a time, without looking down, holding onto your horse's mane, leaning on his neck, hanging on his mouth, or falling back in the saddle.

- Perform walk-trot, walk-halt, and trot-halt transitions while maintaining secure, centered balance.

- Trot over ground poles, releasing the rein contact correctly before the poles and taking up contact again quietly on the other side of the poles.

If you can make these adjustments without disturbing your horse's gait, speed, rhythm, and balance, your independent aids should be well confirmed.

10

FINDING YOUR BALANCE
IN THE SADDLE, II

The Purpose of These Exercises

Riding correctly without stirrups or reins can help you deepen and strengthen your seat, improve your balance, and develop independent aids. Some riding disciplines emphasize the importance of riding without stirrups in the initial stages of a rider's education, but even the most experienced riders often abandon these exercises after they've passed the beginner stage. Eventually, bad habits creep in, and many riders don't realize that they're relying on the stirrups—or even worse, the reins!—for balance.

To make your horse's burden (you) as light as possible, and to effectively offer your horse the rewards of balance, rest, and release from pressure, you need to be able to use your aids promptly, correctly, and independently, and independent aids can be applied only when you ride from a deep, secure base of support. That's what frequent work without stirrups can give you.

So if you've been riding for a long time, use these exercises as a little test to see if you can still maintain that steady seat without the support of stirrups. And if you haven't yet logged thousands of hours in the saddle, these exercises should be an essential part of your training routine.

The arm and shoulder exercises are also helpful as warm-up stretches at the beginning of each ride.

What's in the Rewards Toolbox?

Try to do these exercises as quietly, steadily, and smoothly as possible so that you don't upset your horse's balance or rhythm. Let your horse just carry you around, and don't worry about how he's going as long as he's steady and quiet. Reward your patient horse frequently so he knows he's doing a good job for you.

Ultimately, the best reward for the horse is a lighter, more supple, more secure rider. More immediate rewards include:

- Release of pressure and restoration of balance
- Rest breaks
- Your positive, approving voice
- Appreciative pats and withers rubs

What Do You Need?

You'll need a steady, trustworthy horse who won't be bothered by swinging arms and strange body positions, a round pen to ride in or an experienced friend to longe you, and a comfortable well-fitted dressage or all-purpose saddle with the stirrups pulled off or crossed in front of you. If you usually ride in a western stock saddle and your horse doesn't mind the stirrups dangling at his side, you can use that saddle, but your work will be more effective (and more enjoyable) if you use a well-balanced dressage saddle.

If you're one of those few and fortunate people whose horse travels in a straight, steady, round frame without sidereins, you can leave them off, but I prefer to use sidereins for this exercise. The sidereins help the horse stay straight, balanced, and round in his frame so that his back lifts instead of hollowing. A round horse uses his back more effectively, so his trot and canter are easier to sit.

Be sure your horse is calm, quiet, well warmed up, and strong enough in his back to carry you in a sitting trot before you tackle these exercises. Limit your sessions to 20 or 30 minutes, and take frequent rest breaks as rewards for your horse so he doesn't become fatigued.

Step One

Prepare your horse for longeing by removing or crossing the stirrups, adding sidereins (equal length, no tighter than necessary to keep your horse's head just outside the vertical), securing the reins as shown in the photo on page 57, and attaching the longe line (if you're using one) to the bridle.

Mount up and settle yourself into the saddle with an erect seat and a long leg. Check your position—keep your shoulders back, your chest forward, your head up, and your torso vertical. Be sure there's equal weight on both seatbones, and don't slump back onto your buttocks or collapse your shoulders. Your feet should be directly under you, with toes pulled up and feet steady but not stiff.

Try to keep a long leg with a slight angle at your hips, knees, and ankles. Keep a steady, neutral, wet-clinging-towel feeling with your lower legs against the horse's sides, and don't lift or pinch your knees.

Start walking, and once your horse settles into his rhythm on the longe or in the round pen, begin the arm exercises.

1. Hold both arms straight in front of you at shoulder height for 10 seconds, then raise them straight over your head. Hold for 10 seconds, then lower your left arm to shoulder height while keeping your right arm straight overhead. Switch positions, lowering the vertical one to shoulder height and raising the other. After 10 seconds, drop both arms straight down so your fingers drop to the back of your thighs, directly below your hips.

2. Still at the walk, cross your hands in front of your chest and ride "without arms." Be sure to keep sitting erect; don't slump or collapse in the chest. Now ride with your arms crossed behind your back. (This is an excellent exercise for riders who collapse their chest and shoulders forward.)

3. With arms straight out to the side at shoulder height again, twist your body to the right by turning at the waist, not the hips. Hold for 10 seconds, then twist to the left. Keep your legs steady and even, with no shift in your seat or hips.

For each exercise, it's helpful to have a mirror handy or have a friend check your position. Can you do these upper-body exercises without shifting your legs and seat? Do your shoulders remain square and your back straight? When you drop your arms straight down, do your hands drop directly below your hips? Are you staying straight in the saddle, with equal weight on both seatbones? You should be able to answer yes to all these questions at the walk, before moving on to trot work.

Step Two

Pick up a steady trot, and work to sit straight, steady, and with no bounce. The key to sitting the trot is to stay relaxed—you can't force your way into it, you can't grip your way into it, and you can't slump back on your tailbone. Instead, concentrate on stretching down with your legs and stretching up with your upper body, and ask your abdominal muscles to perform little mini-crunches with each step, helping your seat to rise and fall with the horse's back while your shoulders remain steady. To let your seat follow effectively, your lower back and hips must remain supple—not braced and stiff—so they can work together like a well-oiled hinge.

Richard Valcourt

Richard Valcourt

Emily stretches up through her torso and arms, down through her seat and legs. Her arms could be a little straighter, but her erect, relaxed posture and long, quiet legs are good.

With arms crossed in front of her, Emily must remain straight and steady in the saddle without using her arms and hands for balance. Her seat is centered and deep yet light, and her horse is happy to carry her in a relaxed walk with a stretched topline.

Richard Valcourt

Richard Valcourt

Emily has lifted her knee here and displaced her leg slightly, but she's still well-centered at the trot. Placing her arms behind her back helps her open her shoulders for a straight, tall torso. Riding in this position requires trust in your horse and trust in your own ability to balance without needing to grab the reins or pommel.

Try to maintain the position of your legs and hips as you twist at the waist with your arms horizontal. Emily's shoulders are even, her legs are where they belong, and her weight is even on both seatbones, so her horse continues to travel straight.

Breathe and let go of the tension. Instead of clamping yourself onto the saddle, allow your hip joints to open and close—you need this movement to follow the movement of the horse.

To begin with, leaning back a little behind the vertical (sitting on your pockets) can help you find those stomach muscles. Don't make a habit of this, however, because a habitually heavy, roached, leaning-back posture creates a heavy, ineffective seat. Your goal is to sit on the front of your seatbones, not your buttocks.

Keep the trot slow if sitting is a problem, and keep the sessions short. When you can sit comfortably at a slow trot, staying in balance and rhythm with quiet legs and minimal bouncing, ask your horse to move into a slightly stronger trot to increase the challenge.

Step Three

Now, move from a sitting trot to a posting trot and back again. Alternate with one longe circle of sitting trot, one circle of posting trot, and so on. The posting trot will tell you how strong your legs really are and will help you identify the muscles you *do not* want to grip with when sitting the trot.

To post without stirrups, you do get to grip, though. Tighten your lower thighs, inner knees, and upper calves (but not the lower calves!), and raise your seat about an inch out of the saddle, then sit softly on the next step of the trot. Remember that the goal is not to develop a viselike grip in your legs but to identify and strengthen the leg muscles that will keep you balanced and secure in the saddle.

Then, when you go back to sitting trot, you're going to *let go* of those muscles because, when you sit, those muscles can help you re-center your balance in the saddle—but not if they're busy gripping.

To move smoothly from posting trot to sitting trot, bring your shoulders back closer to the vertical and lower your posting a little with each step until you're barely rising from the saddle. Then relax, engage the abdominal muscles, and let your seat rise and fall with the horse.

Step Four

At the sitting trot, perform the same exercises that you did at the walk.

Give yourself and your horse frequent breaks, and remember that one of the best rewards you can offer to your horse is a light, balanced, supple, easy-to-carry rider. If you're exhausted, you're going to become a much heavier burden for him.

Friction, Balance, and Grip

"Hang on with your knees, not your heels!" my mother told me when I was 4 years old. I learned a lot about horses from her, but she wasn't exactly accurate about the knee-grip part. (Though, in all fairness, it's hard to explain balance and muscle function to a 4-year old.)

Riders sometimes say that riding without stirrups improves their grip so they can stay in the saddle. That's not quite correct: You can't stay in the saddle by gripping with your thighs and knees because those parts of your leg are above the widest point of the horse's barrel, at least for the average-size horse and average-size rider. Gripping with your thighs squeezes you right off the top of the horse—that's how you post without stirrups.

And you can't stay on by gripping with the part of your leg that hangs *below* the widest point of the horse's barrel because then you are gripping with your lower calves, and any sensitive, sensible horse won't put up with *that* for very long. Besides, if you try to stay on by grip alone, you will quickly tire your muscles to the point of failure. So what keeps you in place on a horse? Balance and friction. (And, yes, *sometimes* grip.)

How do you develop balance? Practice, plus the development of your staying-in-place muscles so you can move with your horse and keep your center of gravity over his center of gravity, which is shifting with every step. As the horse moves, your muscles (particularly the thigh, abdominal, and lower-back muscles) must constantly adjust your balance to stay centered over the horse's constantly shifting center of balance. That's why riding for the handicapped works as therapy: The muscles we use to keep our balance while riding are some of the same muscles we also use to keep our balance while standing and walking, though without the weight-bearing demands on our legs and feet.

What about friction? The larger the amount of your body's surface area that rests against the saddle, the more friction you've got working for you. Hence the admonition to ride off the inside of your leg, instead of the back of your leg. The insides of the thigh and calf are wider and flatter than the more-rounded back of the leg. Riding with your toes forward instead of out also keeps the inside of the knee against the saddle, where it can provide additional friction-producing surface area.

And, of course, the nature of the surface matters as well. No one enjoys trying to keep her balance while sliding around on a slick, stiff saddle. On the other hand, some synthetic saddles and full-seat breeches can work like Velcro, locking the rider into such a secure position that she has to peel herself off the saddle to apply a leg aid or change position.

Real grip should come into play only when your horse makes an abrupt shift in balance—when, for example, he shies, stumbles, bucks, or jumps. Then the lower-thigh and upper-calf muscles can be very useful—but only to help you restore your balance and catch up with your horse, not to provide continuous security.

11

Go, Stop, Engage

The Purpose of These Exercises

A willing, sensitive horse responds promptly and without resistance to his rider's requests. If your horse is less than pleasantly responsive, or if he sprawls on his forehand, lacks impulsion, or hangs on your hands during transitions, use these exercises to regain his respect and engagement as you also show him that pleasing you will bring him consistent, reliable rewards.

This seems both simple and self-evident, but there are many horses who have never learned to move forward, speed up, slow down, or halt calmly—and *promptly*—when asked.

Please note that *prompt* doesn't mean *abrupt*. We're talking about calm, relaxed responsiveness, not leaping forward or sliding to a stop. A horse is a dynamic, half-ton animal; his large mass and all four legs need to be rebalanced and organized before he can make adjustments in gaits and tempo. It's important that your horse *begin* to answer your request the moment you ask it, but he needs time and space—from several steps to half a circuit of the arena, depending on his conformation and level of training—to *complete* his response. If he is listening to your aids and *begins* responding right away, then you've achieved prompt obedience, and that's the first step toward engagement of the hindquarters, which is necessary for self-carriage and lightness.

What's in the Rewards Toolbox?
- Your approval and appreciation for his prompt response
- Prompt release of pressure
- Better balance and agility
- Frequent rest breaks

Colin McIver

Willa, a 17-hand Swedish warmblood with "uphill" conformation, backs off contact with the bit by shortening her steps and tucking her head inside the vertical. Rachel keeps her legs and seat active and asks Willa to step forward and stretch a little more . . .

What Do You Need?

You need yourself and your horse, tacked up and ready to ride. This exercise requires contact on the reins, so be sure to use a snaffle or the Bitless Bridle—not a curb, gag, or kimberwicke (unless it's adjusted for snaffle action, with a loose curb chain). If you commonly ride in a pelham or double bridle, be sure that your contact comes through the snaffle rein, not the curb.

A long dressage whip can also help you emphasize your forward requests. The long whip is excellent for schooling because you can touch your horse's hindquarters without taking a hand off the reins or pulling on his mouth as you tap with the whip.

Spurs may be necessary as well, but *only* use spurs if you are absolutely sure your legs are rock-solid steady and you won't poke or grab the horse by mistake. When in doubt, leave them off! A whip is far preferable as reinforcement for the forward aids because if you get in trouble and find yourself on

Richard Valcourt

. . . and when Rachel asks for the trot, Willa obliges by accepting steady but still light contact from Rachel's hands. Rachel has maintained a nice straight line from her elbow to the horse's mouth, no matter where Willa's head goes.

a too-forward horse, you can always drop the whip, but it's hard to take the spurs off when your horse is bolting across the arena in response to a too-sharp application.

Step One

Begin by walking on a loose rein, letting your horse stretch and stroll. Then gradually take up contact with him in a quiet, unobtrusive manner so he accepts it willingly. As you pick up contact, notice his response. Does he slow down and stop the moment you touch the reins? If so, use your legs to send him energetically forward. Does he anticipate and break into a jog? If so, give a quick hold-and-release on the reins to set him back into a walk, then sneak up on the contact again.

Sometimes you simply have to use a very strong command to say "stop." Here Lisa demonstrates the double-and-stop (similar to the pulley rein) on Leo Bar Nani. In the next instant, she'll release the hold to reward her mare.

Your goal here is to have your horse continue walking forward, while at the same time turning his attention to you. As you pick up a little contact from a no-contact state, he should soften his jaw, accept the contact, and perhaps shorten his frame a little in response to the feel of your hands, but he should *continue marching forward.* All you've done is open the lines of communication, his mouth to your hands. This is just quiet contact, not a request for action; you're not actually asking him to do anything yet.

If he tosses his head or pulls on the reins at the slightest contact, don't pull back but don't throw the reins away, either. Keep your hands in quiet, passive contact, follow his head wherever it goes, and keep both legs on (and tap with the whip if necessary) to keep him going forward. The *moment* he stops fussing or relaxes and drops his head, *even just a little*, release the contact and reward him with your voice or a pat, but *don't release until* he gives at least a token of the correct response. You may need to add sliding sidereins (see page 58) to help him find that even, stretchy contact if he sprawls heavily in your hand or flings his head up and goes hollow through his back. Sliding sidereins will also help a ewe-necked horse learn how to strengthen the correct muscles so the transitions become easier for him.

If your horse curls his neck up and puts his chin on his chest to avoid contact altogether, you have a different problem. First, push him forward to encourage him to stretch and use his neck for balance, then ask for light contact, hold it for a few steps, then immediately drop it and give him a pat. He's evading the bit because of past painful experiences and needs to be reassured that you won't hurt him with your hands. This curled-neck evasion impresses some people because the horse appears to have a pretty headset, but it is very different from the lightness and self-carriage that we eventually want our horses to have. Horses with this problem often benefit from being ridden with the Bitless Bridle (see page 72).

Be sure you maintain a light, elastic feel on the reins with your hands, following the motion of the walk without trying to influence it. Each step of the walk requires a telescoping action of the horse's head and neck—he's got to lift and swing that neck to counterbalance each step of his forefeet—and some large, athletic horses can put a lot of movement into their neck motion. If your hands and forearms need to travel six inches forward and back to maintain contact with each step, so be it—you'll know your elbows aren't locked if you can keep passive contact with that kind of walk!

Once you've picked up the contact, begin guiding your horse through turns and corners, helping him bend with your inside leg at the girth to maintain energy and keep him from falling in on his turns. Your inside hand should be asking for the front-end bend, your outside hand supporting and limiting the bend of the neck, and your outside leg back behind the girth to create the bend in the body and keep the hindquarters on the track. Keep your horse marching along in regular rhythm. Follow the motion with your seat, but don't wiggle, bump, push, or otherwise try to influence him with your seat. This is a listen-to-the-leg exercise in going forward.

Be careful how you use your legs! Leg aids should mean something, so your legs should be still and quiet (a reward) when you don't need to say anything. Use your legs to remind your horse to keep the same rhythm when you bend him through corners or on a circle—but if you are nagging him with kicking heels, bumping calves, and swinging legs at every step to *please keep going*, then you need to develop a new system of communication because he's not listening. Ask once, then use your whip to reinforce your request. Ask again with your legs, and reward the correct response by keeping your legs and whip quiet. Don't let the whip become a crutch, either. Always use the whip *after* your correct request from the legs, never *instead of* the leg aids.

Step Two

Now practice halting from the walk. First, *soften* the aids for an instant so that you create a moment of silence. This is your alert signal with which you start your request. You're saying "please." Then bring your legs against your horse's sides again in quiet, passive contact, halt your seat by using your abdominal muscles to lift your torso, and stop following the walk motion in your seat (but don't lean back or brace). Keep your feet back and close your thighs and knees. Say "whoa." *Then* complete the request and ask your horse to stop by bringing your hands back toward your hips. Don't jerk, but hold for no more than one second, and *immediately* release your hands forward to the previous light-contact position, even if your horse hasn't come to a complete stop. Repeat the verbal command plus the release-comeback-release motion of your hands as many times as you need to until he stops completely.

Most horses will complete the halt within three requests. Think of your three requests as the three phases of closing a door: Take hold of the handle, swing it shut, and latch it. If your horse needs more than three requests, fine. Don't escalate your demands or pull harder; simply keep repeating the request and the release until he stops. Or steer straight toward the arena fence or barn wall and ask him to stop when he has a clear reason to do so. Patience is a virtue!

This exercise uses some of the principles of a half-halt, but in a half-halt (or a true halt) you'd be looking for more engagement from the hind end. All we're looking for right now is a responsive stop from the horse, without the rider yanking or hanging on the reins.

Practice this several times until the horse walks forward with energy and halts promptly whenever he's asked. Eventually, you should find yourself using less and less leg pressure to maintain the walk and less and less hand pressure to get the halt.

Then it's time to refine the requests. Instead of moving your hands backward to ask for a halt, simply close the fingers a little and promptly release. Make the three-part halt request both a little more subtle and a little more rapid so that the three requests are completed within three steps: Your aids are saying "Alert, thank you. Halt, thank you. Confirm the halt, thank you." If you've been using your voice as part of your request to halt, trying halting without using your voice. And reward every reasonable attempt your horse makes to comply!

Step Three

Now move on to walk-trot transitions. Say "please" with a moment of silence again in which you quiet everything—hands, legs, seat—for a single step or a single heartbeat. Then ask for forward with light contact on the reins and a light squeeze of your calves. Remember, if you ask for forward and your horse gives you *too much* forward, be careful not to correct him sharply, especially if he's the sluggish type. Don't punish a prompt response! Simply ride quietly and ease him back gently so he can find his balance and relax into a quieter tempo. And if he ignores the politely applied legs, go to the whip.

Again, your horse should move off promptly when asked and then *sustain* the gait and tempo (speed) you ask for. Your goal is stabilization, in which the horse bears the responsibility for maintaining the gait and tempo until you ask for something different. Of course, you have a responsibility, too: You must confirm his correct responses with quiet following aids and not interfere with all attempts on his part to understand and obey.

To return to the walk, lighten your aids, then bring the legs back on, still your seat, and close your hands, then release immediately. If your horse ignores your request to slow down—or if he drops his head and plows forward—ask again, but this time brace your back more strongly and give a quick, sharp, upward tug and release with your inside hand. (The release must be as quick as the tug.) This is not subtle riding and it is not correct riding, but your horse *must* pay attention when you ask him to downshift. He must *also* receive your praise, release, and rest as very clear rewards when he complies—the stronger the request, the bigger the reward.

An even sharper method of enforcing a request to stop is the old-fashioned pulley rein, in which the rider fixes the outside hand on the withers and pulls sharply up and back toward her opposite shoulder with the inside hand, then releases quickly. Another method is the double-and-stop or hitchhiker rein, in which one hand pulls up, back, and out to the side to bring the disobedient horse's nose around almost to the rider's knee.

These very drastic rein effects work because they are abrupt and unexpected and because they throw the horse sharply off balance. They should be used *only* as last-ditch corrective measures for horses who, through poor training or an occasional display of excess and possibly dangerous energy, have learned to pull or hang on a rider's hand while ignoring a reasonable request to slow down. And these methods can be effective *only* if the rider is centered securely in the saddle, keeps her elbows close to her sides, and *releases quickly after the pull*. Otherwise, you'll just teach your horse a new style of tug-of-war.

When you do get a prompt, quiet, downward transition—even if it's unbalanced and disorganized—reward! Relax your aids, use your voice to praise your horse, give lots of nice pats, and let him rest a bit. Don't make any additional demands until you've provided praise for the action he's just performed. You *must* provide positive feedback for each step of the process. Positive horse training always gives a positive reward immediately after a corrective action.

Step Four

If you're riding with a crop or dressage whip to encourage your horse forward, you'd normally carry it in your inside hand to reinforce the aids from your inside leg. However, for canter transitions, switch sides and carry it in your outside hand so it can reinforce your outside leg if your horse is inclined to ignore the signal to canter.

When you ask for a transition into canter, be sure your aids clearly state, "canter on the left lead" or "canter on the right lead," not just "go faster." Prepare by asking for the correct bend, support your horse with your inside leg, then lighten the inside hand and clearly request the canter with your outside leg by cuing for the departure as the horse's outside hind leg is about to leave the ground. That outside hind leg takes the first step to initiate a canter stride, so you need to feel what it is doing.

Here's a simple way to time your request for the canter: If you're trotting and posting on the correct diagonal, your horse's outside hind leg is about to leave the ground when you are coming down into the saddle. So, if you sit and *immediately* ask for the canter, you should be cuing that outside hind leg as it's pushing off. (This also works if you sit two extra steps and then ask. Think of the rhythm as being up, down, up, down, down, *ask*.) If you're in sitting trot, think about what the rhythm would be if you were posting on the correct diagonal, and ask for the canter in your virtual coming-down phase.

Of course, if your horse ignores or follows your cue sluggishly, you won't get a prompt canter no matter how well you time it. Add a tap with your stick behind your *outside* leg to reinforce your request for a prompt canter.

And when you get a prompt canter departure, reward your horse! Maintain the canter, but let him stretch, praise him, give him pats or a quick two-fingered rub on the withers, and let him know as many ways as you can that you are pleased! Tell him immediately how happy you are with his attempts to listen so that he'll be inclined to repeat his correct response for you.

12

SQUARES, OCTAGONS, CIRCLES

The Purpose of These Exercises

Most trainers spend many hours working on corners and circles because correctly executed turns and circles can help horses develop balance, correct bending, straightness (equal suppleness and strength on both sides), and hind-end engagement. Constantly trying to perfect the absolutely round circle, however, can have a mind-numbing effect on both horse and rider. Riders struggle to keep their horses from falling in on the inside shoulder, drifting out with the haunches, counterbending or overbending in the neck, rushing, or simply refusing to steer. They often seem to think they need to ride a circle by micromanaging it and holding their horses clamped between their legs and hands to create a consistent bend and a perfectly round circle.

In fact, a correctly ridden circle (or any turn) happens step by step, just like every other action in riding, in a nearly constant interplay of request-response-reward. This series of exercises takes the circle apart by starting with 90-degree corners and straight lines. It clarifies the role of the rider's aids in the request-response-reward cycle and clearly explains to the horse how he can work for the rewards of better balance and comfort.

This is an excellent way to strengthen your young horse's understanding of the concepts of steering, bending, and accepting the aids. For the more experienced horse, riding 90-degree turns at trot and canter will help him find his balance, engage his hind legs, and lighten his forehand. These exercises should also help you learn how to better help your horse balance and bend on turns, *without* you holding him up, in, and together at every step.

What's in the Rewards Toolbox?

- Your verbal approval and pats of appreciation
- A very clear and prompt release of pressure from the aids
- Improved balance and agility
- Being able to rebalance on a straight line after turning a corner
- Rest and relaxation

What Do You Need?

You need your horse, yourself, and your usual tack. As with the previous exercises under saddle, these exercises require contact on the reins. Use a simple snaffle, the Bitless Bridle, or a pelham or kimberwicke in snaffle mode. (With a kimberwicke, this means you should undo the curb chain or make it as loose as possible and place the rein in the top slot. With a pelham, remove or tie up the curb rein so it's out of your way.)

You'll also need some way of marking off a square in your arena. Use eight ground poles (two at each corner to form 90-degree angles), place several cones at each corner, or mark lines on the ground with lime to create a square that's at least 50 feet wide. A 66-foot square is even better. Be sure the corners are square, the ground is level, and both you and your horse can clearly see the markers.

Step One

After you and your horse are sufficiently warmed up, take up a medium walk with light contact and begin walking along one side of the square. Start in the direction in which you both feel most comfortable (for most horses, this will be counterclockwise). Keep your horse marching forward energetically, but don't let him rush.

As you approach the first corner, don't let your horse anticipate the turn or cut the corner. Instead, halt on a straight line a few steps before you get to the corner. Use equal pressure on both reins or slightly more on the outside rein if your horse has a tendency to shift his shoulders inward to avoid facing the barrier in the corner. The halt will prepare him for the turn by shifting his balance back onto his hindquarters and remind him not to rush in an attempt to cut the corner and get through the turn quickly if he's unbalanced. Be sure to keep both your legs in contact to hold him straight.

Then ask him to walk forward again and turn the corner by using an inside leading or opening rein. Your inside leg should be on the horse's girth, giving little squeezes in rhythm with the walk, and your outside leg should be placed a little behind the girth to keep his hindquarters from swinging out. (If you're riding close to a fence line or other horse-height barrier, you shouldn't need much outside leg to keep him in place.) Your outside hand should be close to his neck in steady contact, both to limit the bend in his neck and to direct his shoulders into the turn.

As you come three or four steps out of the corner, reward! Lighten both reins a little, and invite your horse to stretch for a few steps. Keep him stepping forward as straight as possible, however, by keeping your legs and seat active if he's a little sluggish. Horses tend to slow down in turns because they have to work a little harder to change balance as they stretch the outside of their bodies, contract the inside, and carry more weight on the inside hind leg. So if you want your horse to keep moving at a consistent speed and rhythm from a straight line through a turn and back to a straight line again, you'll probably have to add energy for the turn and steady him on the straightaways. (This is why circling is a traditional method of stopping a runaway.)

If your horse tends to quicken coming out of the turn and wants to rush down the straight side of your square, make your release reward brief and then quietly take up contact and ask him to halt for a moment. Give a release reward for the halt, then let him walk forward again.

A variation of this exercise is to perform the 90-degree turn with a quarter-turn on the forehand or on the haunches. For green horses, the halt-turn-halt exercise is plenty challenging enough, but a more experienced horse will bene-fit from the additional lateral request. Just be sure you've allowed enough room on your turns for your horse to swing his haunches to the outside if you ask for a turn on the forehand. (See chapter 13 for more information about how to ride turns on the forehand and turns on the haunches.)

What Is Steady Contact?

Steady contact never means fixed, unyielding contact. Steady contact is *following* contact. This means the rider has a consistent feel of the horse's mouth and the rider's hands feel steady and consistent to the horse. The horse's head and neck are moving almost constantly, in motions and rhythms that change with gait, speed, balance, and occasional outside influences. The rider's hands must be able to follow all of these movements, no matter where the horse's head goes or how abruptly it gets there.

There are two secrets to maintaining steady, elastic, sensitive rein contact: a deep, secure, balanced seat and relaxed arms that can act independently from the rest of your body. The only way to acquire independent hands is to learn how to keep your balance on a moving horse, no matter what that horse does or where he goes. An independent seat and good balance, however, aren't enough. Locked elbows, stiff wrists, clenched fists, and tight shoulders will all hinder your ability to follow and support your horse's movements without inhibiting them.

The solution? Many, many hours in the saddle, especially working without stirrups and balancing in two-point position. See chapters 9 and 10 for suggestions on improving your balance.

Step Two

Repeat your walk exercise a few times in each direction, riding the corners with a halt-release-walk-turn-release (and perhaps another halt-release) pattern. As your horse becomes more responsive to your aids, you can eliminate the full halts and substitute half-halts. That is, going into the corner, momentarily close your inside leg a little more firmly as you tighten the feel on the outside rein. Immediately release and allow the walk, then lead into the turn, and as you come out of the turn, repeat the half-halt with the inside-leg–outside-rein action.

One note about timing: A very important concept in this exercise is to ask for the rebalancing halt or half-halt *before* you ask for the bend and to create the bend *before* you ask for the turn. Perform your halt or half-halt for a few strides before you ask for the bend, then ask for the bend at least two strides before the turn. Keep your inside leg firmly in place to keep your horse on the track so that he doesn't fall in or cut the corner.

When your horse is completing these turns nicely in both directions at the walk, pick up the sitting or rising trot and repeat the exercise. (The sitting trot is best because your weight remains centered in the saddle and you can use your seat more effectively to influence your horse's rhythm and balance. But if you're not steady and secure in the sitting trot, by all means post!)

At the trot, don't perform halt transitions before and after each corner unless your horse is fairly well schooled and well balanced in his trot-halt transitions on straight lines. Instead, use a series of inside-leg-to-outside-hand half-halts before each corner to help him rebalance and engage his hindquarters. Six steps before the corner, half-halt three times, at every other step, as your horse's inside hind leg lifts off the ground (as you rise out of the saddle at the posting trot). Then guide him through the corner, reward, use a few more half-halts to help him find his balance on the straight line, and reward again with a little release followed by steady, quiet contact.

The great thing about half-halts is that every half-halt, when done correctly, has a reward built into it: You press the horse forward into your hand and *immediately* release on the next step, even *before* the horse has finished responding to the request for a little more engagement.

Why is the square so effective in helping horses and riders find their balance in turns? Because the bending/turning request is brief and very clearly defined, and the reward (of traveling in a straight line on light contact) follows almost automatically. If the horse has trouble balancing on his turns, he can very quickly regain his balance on the straightaway without feeling he has to rush or struggle.

Step Three

Now for the approximate octagon. Remember your basic geometry? A square has four sides, an octagon has eight, and a circle can be thought of as having an infinite number of sides. So we can think about riding a circle by starting with a square, then adding straight lines and reducing the sharpness of each corresponding angle.

Why should we do this? Because turns can be tough on a horse's balance. From the horse's point of view, each turn is a task and each straight line is a reward—so one good way to help a horse find his balance is to make the turns brief and to include a straight line as a reward for each turn. If we think first of riding a square, then an octagon, then a dodecagon (12 sides), and (eventually) a circle, we can break the task down into request-reward pieces. In a well-executed circle, one step contains the task and the next contains the reward, but the communication between horse and rider is so subtle that a spectator may not see the difference.

For a work area, you can use the square you laid out in step one. Some people like to arrange ground poles in an octagon pattern to help guide them, but you can also simply envision the octagon pattern in your mind. I like to lay out poles in this pattern:

To ride an octagon, first ask your horse to walk as perfect a circle as possible (at least 50 feet in diameter). Count the number of strides your horse takes to complete the circle at a walk. Depending on their size and conformation, most horses will take 28 to 40 strides to complete a 66-foot diameter circle at the walk. Let's say your horse makes his way around in 32 strides; that means each side of the octagon could be ridden in four walking strides (32 ÷ 8 = 4). Begin your walk around again, but this time ride an approximate octagon: Go straight for three strides, half-halt, and ask for a 45-degree turn for one stride, go straight for three strides, turn for one, and so on.

At the walk, Rachel bends Willa through the corner of the square with an active inside leg, a supportive outside hand and leg, and a leading inside rein. Willa has responded by shortening her steps and yielding with a soft jaw. Rachel's inside leg should be stretched down more to apply the aid from the calf instead of the heel. Still, she's looking where she's going, her shoulders are square, and she's maintained sensitive contact with a straight line from her elbow to Willa's mouth. When she comes out of the corner . . .

It doesn't matter if you don't finish the pattern in precisely eight turns or if you've miscalculated the number of strides your horse takes to get all the way around. It also doesn't matter if the turns don't happen at the same place each time you go around your octagon. The important thing is to set up a steady rhythm of tasks (half-halts and turns) and rewards (releases and straight lines) that *don't* demand constant, heavy hands and continuous pushing or prodding by the rider or a heavy, leaning, falling-to-the-inside position by the horse.

Be sure to work both directions, beginning with your horse's easy side but concentrating a little more on his difficult side.

Richard Valcourt

. . . Rachel gives Willa two rewards: a very obvious release of the rein aids and a straight walk forward. I'd like to see Willa stretch down and forward more, but she is relaxed, quiet, and attentive to her rider.

Step Four

After you've established the approximate octagon pattern at the walk, pick up a trot, using a three-stride rhythm: Every three strides, ask for the half-halt, bend, and turn, then allow the horse to go straight for two strides. Everything must happen faster now, with the half-halt and the request for the bend combined so they occur almost simultaneously. So now your aids for the turn will be inside leg into outside hand (half-halt) with an inside leading rein (turn request); an instant later, you relax the aids and allow the horse to straighten. Then, two strides later, ask again.

As your horse becomes stronger and better balanced through all of this turning, his improved balance also becomes his reward, and he should find these

Richard Valcourt

Emily asks Coosa Lani to bend through the corner at a trot. Emily has
raised her inside hand very slightly and is using a strong inside leg, plus
a supportive outside rein, to counter this mare's tendency to lean over
her inside shoulder on the turn. Here we can clearly see the engagement
and carrying power of the horse's inside leg, which is reaching well
underneath her body. In the next step, Emily will use a half-halt to
straighten and rebalance and will then reward Coosa Lani by lightening
all the aids and allowing her to travel straight ahead for a few strides,
until they prepare for the next corner.

exercises much easier. He can't hang on to your inside rein or allow you to hold him up because the moment after you've requested the bend and turn, you've released the inside rein. Be sure he continues to go forward off your leg at both the walk and the trot.

Step Five

After you've mastered the octagon, a true circle should be easy. Simply refine your requests for the half-halt, bend, and turn by combining them into a command in one step, and give a subtle release reward in the next step. At the two-beat trot, you should *request* as the horse's inside hind leg pushes off the ground (as you rise if you're posting to the trot) and *release* as it lands.

When you've confirmed a balanced circle at the trot, move on to a canter in your square and approximate octagon patterns. Be careful, however, not to ask a green or unbalanced horse to go too deep into his corners; he may be easily frightened if he's not yet capable of rocking back on his hocks for a tight turn. For most horses, establishing good balance is much harder at the canter than at the trot. Enlarge your circle, round off your corners so they're not too sharp, but stay with the same concept of corner/task, alternating with straightaway/reward. Watch for any tendency to rush, scramble, or fall in on the corners, and return to a slower gait at the first sign of trouble.

If your horse does tend to drop his inside shoulder and lean around corners, first be sure *your* weight is correctly centered and you're not contributing to his imbalance by dropping your inside shoulder, leaning to the inside, falling ahead of the motion, dropping your eyes, or hanging on his mouth. Keep a little more weight in your outside stirrup, and keep your outside hand low. Then slow down, reestablish your horse's balance going into the turn by using a few more inside-leg-to-outside-hand half-halts, and try lifting your inside shoulder and hand an inch as you ask for the bend. This does two things: It reminds you to avoid collapsing the inside of your body and helps your horse keep his head straight and his inside shoulder up.

13

LATERAL YESWORK, NOT GUESSWORK

The Purpose of These Exercises

It's critical for a rider to be able to control the position and activity of the whole horse, especially the hindquarters. To propel himself forward, a horse must push off his hind end, and to balance a rider's weight, he needs to develop strength and carrying power in the hindquarters. Horses aren't born knowing how to carry a rider, so it's our responsibility to help them develop strength and balance for the work we ask them to do.

Simple lateral exercises such as leg-yielding and turns on the forehand and haunches help develop the horse's agility, balance, and strength. They also create patterns of communication and obedience by reminding the horse that the rider's aids—hands, legs, and weight—communicate sideways movement and positioning, not just brakes, accelerator, and steering.

These skills have some very practical applications, too. Your horse's obedience to lateral aids will get you through a gate, help you steady a snorty horse past a spooky object, and (literally) get you smoothly out of a tight corner.

The rewards for the horse? Good lateral responsiveness and suppleness should improve his balance and strength, so all his work should come a little easier for him. As his job gets easier, your communication can be more subtle, so your horse should feel less pressure and more approval from you.

What's in the Rewards Toolbox?
- As always, your verbal approval and pats of appreciation
- A very clear and prompt release of pressure
- Rest and relaxation
- Improved balance and agility

What Do You Need?

I like to keep things simple, so I'm not going to insist on the classical dressage version of a precise turn on the haunches or a perfect leg-yield, but you do need to have certain basic skills and tools to achieve successful lateral work without confusing your horse or frustrating yourself.

You should be ready to ride in a balanced saddle and snaffle bridle, or bitless equivalent, with your horse nicely warmed up and relaxed. If your horse is a little sluggish or slow to respond to your leg aids, you may want to have a dressage whip and/or spurs handy in case you need to add emphasis to your requests. You'll also need some sort of visible barrier such as a wall, a fence line, or a line of rails set on barrels to limit your horse's forward motion and help him understand why stepping sideways at your direction is an important skill to learn. A right-angle corner of an arena or paddock will also be helpful.

Before you begin this series of exercises under saddle, review the ground-work in chapter 7 to be sure your horse is confirmed in the lateral groundwork described in steps four, five, and six. Before starting lateral work under saddle, you should be able to direct his hindquarters or shoulders to either side with simple hand and halter pressure from the ground.

Now it's time to put these skills to work under saddle.

Step One

We start with a turn on the forehand because it's easier for a green horse who's heavy on the front end to move his back end around his front than vice versa.

Some people don't like to teach a horse turns on the forehand because it contradicts two goals of good riding: establishing *forward* impulsion with weight carried on the *hindquarters*. I believe the turn on the forehand is the easiest way, however, to teach a horse to understand the use of your leg as a sideways-pushing aid. As soon as he understands the idea of pivoting his hind end around his front end, you can move on to leg-yielding, which requires forward motion.

Begin by walking straight toward a fence or other barrier. Ask your horse to stop with his nose about three or four feet away (a little farther back if it's an electric fence because many horses will not want to get that close to the wire, whether it's hot or not!). Be sure he walks straight toward the barrier and halts quietly.

Reward him with a release of pressure for the halt, then quietly pick up the contact in both reins, ask him to flex very slightly to the left by momentarily tightening the left rein a little, and then ask him to move his hindquarters to the right with your left leg. Try to keep your horse's head and neck straight by maintaining contact on both reins. If necessary, you can guide his head to the left a little more with a leading (opening) left rein if he seems clueless about where he's supposed to go.

Essentially, you're asking him to make a 90-degree turn by moving his haunches away from your left leg. Use your leg a couple of inches behind the girth in a pulse action to request the steps you'd like him to take: push-step-relax, push-step-relax. Just ask for his head and neck to swing left and his hindquarters to go right. If he simply stands there and ignores you, get a little more vigorous with your leg or add a tap from your whip (which, of course, you're carrying in your left hand so you can touch him precisely behind your left leg).

Unless your horse tries to step backward, your right leg should be completely passive. A backward step or two can be corrected by momentarily applying both legs to send him forward again, but if he throws his head up and squirms backward or shoots sideways nervously, he's not ready to learn this under saddle. Hop off, and use your hand pressed against his ribcage to ask him to shift his hindquarters away from pressure.

Keep everything quiet, clear, and patient, and reward him with pats and releases as soon as he makes even the smallest attempt to comply. Whether he accomplishes a nice quiet turn on the forehand with his hindquarters pivoting around his front end (your goal), or whether he sort of makes a turn around his middle, reward him immediately by releasing pressure and letting him step out of the turn into a relaxed, straight-ahead walk. Pat, voice your approval, walk quietly around, and repeat the exercise a few times in the same manner.

Step Two

After your horse has mastered a 90-degree turn to the left, change direction and practice the same exercise to the right. Halt in front of a wall or fence, flex him very slightly to the right, and use an active right leg to push his hindquarters to the left. Pay attention to which direction seems to be more difficult for your horse (usually to the right, which is why we began with a turn to the left), and spend a little more time on the "stickier" direction.

Step Three

When you think your horse has the idea of moving his hindquarters away from your leg in a 90-degree turn in either direction while he's facing a wall, try asking for a 180-turn at various places along your arena fence. Be sure you ask for a turn in the correct direction so that his head swings toward the wall or fence and he can see the barrier. If you ask him to turn with his hindquarters toward the fence, he may be concerned about bumping the fence with his tail end. Also, with the barrier *behind* him, he'll see no logical reason for completing a tight turn—he can simply walk forward into the arena and use all the space he needs. If he tries to step forward, close your hands and ask for the halt again, or go back to using the wall or a corner as a visual barrier.

Now you can begin refining your aids a little, asking your horse to pivot more smoothly while his neck and body remain straight. Continue to ask for the slight flexion of his poll just before asking his hindquarters to move, but make it more subtle.

When your horse has mastered the turn on the forehand, you should perform it only once in a while as a sharpening-up exercise. And don't overdrill on these exercises! Some horses will quickly associate the halt with a turn on the forehand. They may start swinging their hindquarters to one side as soon as you halt, in anticipation of a turn on the forehand.

Coosa Lani has just begun a turn on the forehand. Emily has asked for a slight flexion right at the poll as she uses her right leg to send the mare to the left. Coosa has picked up her right front pivot foot and will place it down again in almost the same place; she's also about to take a large step to her left with her left hind leg. Emily could be more effective here if she kept her eyes up and sat more evenly balanced, but she's getting the job done with steady, press-step-release precision.

Bird has asked 3-year-old Joe for the beginning of a turn on the haunches. She's using both hands and her right leg at the girth to direct him to the left. Her left leg is behind the girth to keep his haunches steady. He's just finishing his first step with his left front foot. One or two steps of the turn is enough for this youngster, as his still-developing body tends to be heavy in the forehand.

Willa is offering a nice leg-yield at the walk, with her body remaining straight and her right hind leg showing good reach, as she crosses high up near the hocks. This is a good exercise for this mare because it helps strengthen her back and hindquarters.

At the trot, Willa remains steady on both reins as she leg-yields to the right. I'd like her neck not to be overbent—her poll is not the highest point, as it should be—but she travels straight and accepts a light, calm contact on both reins. Her trot is more forward than this photo indicates.

Be sure to reward your horse frequently with rest and relaxation during lateral work. Lisa encourages Nani Bar Leo to stretch down and forward at the walk.

Step Four

After your horse can manage a reasonable turn on the forehand, move on to leg-yielding. Leg-yielding is a great warm-up exercise because it loosens and stretches each side of the horse's body.

Leg-yielding asks the horse to go forward and sideways simultaneously. In dressage, true leg-yielding requires the horse to move with his body straight but angled at about 35 degrees to his line of travel. There's no bending required in leg-yielding—in fact, we *want* the horse's body to remain straight. Movements that require sideways motion plus bending are difficult for the horse to master, so we keep the bending work separate from the lateral work until the horse has mastered each skill separately.

Start by riding with contact at a walk in a straight line down the center of your arena. Locate a point at the end of your straight line, then shift your eyes about 10 or 15 feet to the right of that point. Flex your horse's head *just a little* to the left at the poll with your left hand, and keep contact with the right rein so he doesn't bend his neck left. Try to keep his body straight as you ride toward that point at the end of the arena by pushing a little with your left leg in rhythm with the walk, timing it so your leg pushes a little each time your horse's left hind leg pushes off the ground.

You're asking for just a *little* angle and just a *few* steps sideways/forward. The moment you feel the horse's left hind leg reach under him a little more as his body shifts sideways, reward! Give your horse a pat, release the reins, and let him stretch and walk straight ahead.

Repeat the same exercise in the other direction. Every horse and every rider has a stronger and a weaker side, so you'll want to spend a little more time on the direction that's more difficult for both of you. Remember:

- Slow the walk down if it's quick or strong. Leg-yielding requires your horse to engage his hindquarters, and he can't do that if he's rushing along on his forehand.

- But don't slow it down too much! Try to keep a steady rhythm—no squirming or hesitating.

- Ask for just a few steps at first, and give lots of rewards so your horse knows when he's done well.

- Stay centered in the saddle. Don't collapse your body, lift your heel, or twist sideways in an effort to get your horse to *move over*. If he's not responding to your leg, add a nudge from a spur or a tap from a whip on the appropriate side. Go back to turns on the forehand to reinforce the move-away-from-the-leg command.

- The biggest mistake in leg-yielding is to overbend the horse's neck and force him to fall over his shoulder. Keep his neck and body straight; he should look only *slightly* away from the direction of travel. Use a slight leading rein to keep his neck from overbending as you send him in the direction of travel. (Use a leading right rein if you're leg-yielding to the right, away from the left leg.)

After your horse can give you a few steps of leg-yield in both directions at the walk, simply ask for a greater angle and more steps in each direction. Then move on to a sitting trot and do the same exercises. Leg-yielding can also be done along the side of the arena in a head-to-the-wall position. If your horse tends to want to run faster every time you use your leg, you may find this easier to teach than leg-yielding down the center because by positioning the horse's head toward the wall, you can help him learn not to rush forward to escape your leg.

Don't practice leg-yielding exercises only in the arena—get out on the trails, and ask your horse to leg-yield along the road or trail. Practice going left-to-right and right-to-left in a zigzag pattern. It's a great way to slow down a too-rapid walker or help a distracted horse focus, and it will also help get you around spooky objects. If you've got a suspicious-looking rock over there on your right, ask your horse to look a little left and use your left leg to send his body closer to the scary object. He'll have to focus on your request, rebalance himself, move away from the leg, and move forward—and *voilá*, you're past the rock.

Step Five

Now it's time to ask your horse to learn a simple turn on his haunches. In classical dressage, a correct turn on the haunches requires the horse to bend evenly in the direction of movement while pivoting on a hind foot and maintaining the rhythm of the gait, but we're not going to get that fancy. We'll just ask the horse to mobilize his shoulders, shift his weight back onto his hindquarters, and turn his front end around his hind end while looking in the direction of his turn.

Before you ask for a turn on the haunches while mounted, your horse should be responsive from the ground. You should be able to shift his shoulders over by pushing his head away a little and applying hand pressure to his shoulders, as described in chapter 7, step five. From the saddle, here's how to introduce a turn on the haunches.

In your arena, ride counterclockwise at a walk along your fence line until you come to a right-angle corner. (If you don't have a right-angle corner, you can build one from poles and barrels or jump standards.) Ride deep into the corner, turn the corner, then halt with your horse's tail as close as possible to the fence behind you. The fence line on your right will help keep his hindquarters from swinging out, and the barrier behind him will help keep him from backing up.

Reward the halt, let him settle for a few seconds, then pick up the rein contact and move both hands to the left. Your left hand leads his head a little left while your right hand creates an indirect or even a bearing rein (neckrein) action, moving to the left and pressing against the right side of his neck in front of the withers, to help swing his shoulders over to the left. Your right leg should be behind the girth, holding the hindquarters in place, and your left leg should press at the girth to encourage the movement.

If the horse seems stuck in place and doesn't understand, ask him to back up a step to put his hindquarters more underneath him, then ask again. (But don't ask him to back so far into the corner that he hits the wall! That's a trust buster—he'll never want to stand in a corner for you again.)

Ask for only one or two steps at first; many horses cannot manage more than this in the beginning. When your horse shifts his shoulders sideways, even a little, reward him! Pat him, speak kindly, and let him walk forward out of the corner and stretch.

Some horses manage the first couple of steps in a turn on the haunches, then get tangled up trying to figure out what to do with their hind legs. If this happens, let him take a step forward and then ask again. And don't insist on a stationary pivot—as long as his front feet go around in a larger arc than his hind feet, that's success.

Use the corners to practice small turns on the haunches in both directions. Then move out of the corners and try the same exercise along the sides of the arena and eventually out in the open with no supporting wall or fence lines. Ask for more steps, gradually working up to a one-quarter or one-half turn. Eventually, you can modify the aids and use the mobilized-shoulders skill to help your horse learn a true turn on the haunches, a pirouette, a rollback, or a sidepass.

Be sure you thoroughly understand your horse's personality and can assess his reactions to these exercises. Lazy horses tend to do well performing turns on the forehand and haunches, but nervous, excitable horses may be upset by them. Ask only for steady, step-by-step compliance—don't encourage your horse to whirl around rapidly or dance sideways. Stay calm, reassure the anxious horse, and move on to something less demanding whenever he shows signs of nervousness. Know his comfort zone, and understand his limitations for every task.

14

OVERHEAD AND UNDERFOOT: COMBAT TRAINING

The Purpose of These Exercises

For horses, the world of people must be a continually puzzling and sometimes terrifying place. When a horse's every instinct tells him to run away from loud noises, fluttering and rustling objects, unsteady footing, and possible predators, we ask him to stand and work quietly.

Combat training (also called bombproofing) is an intensive program to *safely* introduce horses to as many varied and potentially frightening situations as possible, with as many positive results as possible.

To set up a program that asks him to meet and successfully overcome his natural fears, we have to respect the horse's need for safety through flight. In other words, we must not force him into anything he's not ready for. It's critical to make each horse feel safe, encourage him to trust his human leaders, and allow him to use his natural curiosity to learn about new objects and experiences.

Trainers can and should begin small confidence-building exercises very early in a horse's life, literally from birth. Rustling paper, the hiss of a spray can, the sights and sounds of moving bicycles, barking dogs, farm animals, traffic, and noisy children—these are all part of everyday life. If your horse hasn't learned to accept these common experiences—if he lives a secluded, solitary, or unusually regimented life—it's your responsibility as a trainer to seek out or create situations in which you can introduce these basic experiences.

Each time your horse learns to manage a carefully controlled "danger," you'll reward him with your approval. As he learns to look for your guidance in unfamiliar situations, he'll be more willing to accept your leadership in all aspects of your relationship. The larger rewards for both of you should include increased confidence, better trust and communication, and greater safety in potentially scary real-life situations.

What's in the Rewards Toolbox?

- Your enthusiastic approval, pats, and verbal encouragement
- Rest and relaxation
- Food rewards (optional)
- Satisfied curiosity
- Reduced anxiety and increased confidence in new situations

What Do You Need?

Your horse can be almost any age for combat training, but he should be trained to lead politely, stand quietly, and maneuver through simple ground poles (review chapter 7). In most young horses (especially those who haven't had their sense of trust destroyed by rough handling or painful experiences), curiosity is often stronger than fear. Older horses tend to be more suspicious and less interested in exploring their surroundings.

Outfit him with a sturdy halter and a long, thick, cotton lead rope. It's a good idea to wear gloves to prevent a rope burn if he startles or jerks away suddenly. You may also want to have a long stick (about 40 inches) or dressage whip handy, in case you need to help him go forward a little with the tap of a stick. If halter training isn't quite confirmed, have a second long, cotton rope available to sling around his hindquarters if necessary.

To create a full combat training course, you'll also need to collect a lot of interesting items that can be safely looked at, touched, walked on, or listened to by your horse. These might include an umbrella, plastic sheets or big, black trash bags, a wheelbarrow with rakes and shovels to rattle, an old mattress or mattress-size foam pad, balloons, a lawnmower, a bicycle and bicyclist, a boom box with various types of music, old tires, a hose with a lawn sprinkler attached, and some sort of tall outdoor tent or awning that you and your horse can walk into or under. If you don't have a proper tent or awning, you can drape a tarp over a gateway or suspend a plastic sheet about 10 feet off the ground between two trees. Ask a friend to bring his dirt bike, and encourage the neighbor's kids to set up a camping tent in your backyard.

Add to this list anything else you know has caused your horse concern in the past, but remember that your obstacles *must* be safe and sturdy, and take every precaution to make sure your horse will not get hurt.

Consider where your combat training will take place. You can introduce some items and exercises to your horse while he's in his box stall, but save the big, noisy stuff for outdoors. A round pen is the ideal size for most of this work. It's small enough to keep his attention focused on the task but not so small that he'll feel trapped. Do *not* turn him loose in a paddock that contains sharp-edged objects, mechanical equipment, wires, or unbreakable rope; and do not confine him in ا stall with some big, noisy, fear-inducing object that he can't escape from.

Remember that your horse must go through several distinct behaviors before a new object becomes part of his general knowledge and memory. He must:

1. Notice the object.
2. Examine it from a distance with his eyes and ears.
3. Examine it up close with his eyes, ears, touch, smell, and taste.
4. Watch and listen to see if it moves or makes noise or changes in any way.
5. Examine it again when it has changed.

If any one of those behaviors causes him pain or threatens his perception of safety, trust will be destroyed. Each step toward trust on your horse's part must be rewarded somehow—with your approval, a reduction of anxiety, or a satisfaction of his curiosity.

Essentially, you're teaching your horse that when you touch him or when you ask him to touch, look at, step on, or walk by something, *he will not be hurt*. Repeat this basic lesson several times, and you'll develop trust—because he *hasn't* been hurt. (If you do hurt him, even once, even by mistake, you'll have to start all over again. Keep him safe!)

This is one set of exercises in which food rewards can definitely be helpful. Consider keeping lots of small carrot slices in a handy belt pack so you can offer them as rewards as you work through these obstacles.

Step One

In every exercise, you'll go through three phases: First, introduce the object for the horse's inspection. Then add movement or sound as you ask him to stand quietly. Finally, ask the horse to take some action in the direction of the object (follow it, step on it, walk under it).

During each phase, you must pay close attention to your horse's level of comfort. His ears, eyes, body posture, and willingness to approach or stand his ground are going to tell you whether he's inside, just a little outside, or very far away from his comfort zone. As long as he's showing comfort signals (lowered head, relaxed breathing, eyes and ears attentive but relaxed), you can move on. If he shows any signs of anxiety (raised head, snorting or rapid breathing, rolling eyes, trembling, attempts to flee), go back to a previous phase or repeat something he was comfortable with earlier, and find a way to reward him for being as brave as he can be.

several interesting but harmless items in a round pen or small
n him loose to explore. I like to start with a garden hose, a tire,
.ic barrel, a plastic tarp or a mattress, and a plastic trash bag tied
provide pure positive reinforcement by scattering some carrots on
tarp, and tire and then I observe for 10 minutes or so. And *every
time* ... roaches an object to investigate, I reward him with my approval
voice from outside the round pen.

Pay attention to which items he's comfortable with and which ones he
won't go near. A young, curious horse who hasn't been frightened by any of
these objects will check them all out pretty quickly and will probably find
ways to play with them or push them around. An older horse may snort or
sniff at one or two items, then stand a safe distance away and keep a wary eye
on the items he doesn't trust, with an attitude that says, "If I ignore them,
they'll go away."

A nervous horse may simply stand as far away as possible from everything
and wait for someone to take everything away. And a truly fearful horse may try
to escape without displaying the slightest bit of curiosity about anything.

After 10 to 15 minutes of observation, you should be able to tell which
items your horse has accepted and which ones he doesn't like. If he's accepted
or examined everything, great—now you can move on to step two.

If he hasn't freely examined everything in the round pen, clip on your lead
rope and walk him up to each item in turn. If he approaches everything calmly
and simply stands there with a bored expression, move on to step two.
However, if he shows anxiety or resistance about approaching any of the
items, you'll need to focus on those objects. Walk him up to those items that
he will approach willingly; reward with praise, pats, and carrots; let him
watch you place a few more carrots near the other objects; and leave him in
the round pen with all the items for an hour longer. Then ask him again to
approach everything. You can be a little more insistent this time. Carry your
stick behind you, and tap him forward if he plants his feet or twists away. Be
very alert to reward every attempt at compliance. If your horse so much as
puts his head down to look more closely at the item, that's a small success and
deserves a reward.

If you're working with a yearling or a 2-year-old, try introducing these
obstacles in the presence of an older, more experienced horse who will set a
good example. It may also help to drop a butt rope around the baby's rump and
encourage him forward with a few tugs. I've also used backing to encourage a
horse who simply did *not* want to confront anything head-on. We backed toward
each item and executed a quarter-turn on the forehand to place his head closer
to each obstacle. When he could no longer ignore and distrust everything from
a distance, his natural curiosity kicked in and he chose to investigate each item.

Repeat the introductory exercise until he'll follow you to each item and
stand quietly. Then move on to step two.

Step Two

Now you can introduce movement or sound in each of the objects. Begin with an item the horse is thoroughly comfortable with—let's say it's the hose. Turn your horse free in the round pen again. If the space is a little cluttered, you may want to stack other items out of the way. Let him watch as you move them around. Then start playing with the hose. Drag it around; coil it up; stretch it out. Every time your horse shows concern about the movement, stop, retreat a little, and let him explore on his own. Reward with your voice and a carrot. Then go back to playing with the hose.

When he's bored with the movement of the hose, move on to each of the other items and explore the ways you can make them move, shake, rattle, and eventually touch him. If your horse follows you around and is willing to explore everything with you, you can do this without an assistant. But if he's not willing to stand near the rolling barrel or the rustling plastic, ask an assistant to create the movements while you lead your horse a little closer.

Every time your horse resists or asks to retreat, you need to determine whether his response is genuine anxiety or a low-anxiety, general resistance to following your lead. If it's the former, use an approach-retreat method to get him comfortable with everything. Approach him with the strange object as long as he's willing to stand his ground or move toward it; make the object retreat as soon as he backs up or shows anxiety. Then have your assistant roll the barrel or drag the hose *away* from him, and lead your horse behind it. Predators, after all, don't move *away* from a potential meal, so as soon as that blue barrel rolls away from your horse, his comfort level will increase. Obviously, the barrel is not a predator!

If, instead, you feel that your horse is reluctant to participate because he simply doesn't respect your requests—if he leads forward sluggishly and hangs back no matter what you're asking him to do—pick up your dressage whip, place yourself in the position shown in the photo on the top of page 88, and add a tap from the stick to send him forward. Then reward.

Explore all the possibilities of shape and sound and movement, and let your horse watch everything you do. Attach the lawn sprinkler to the hose and turn it on (perhaps just outside the round pen at first, so he can escape the spray if he wants to). Roll the tire and let it bump the barrel. Stuff the hose into the plastic trash bag, or drape it over the fence; then drape it over your horse's back and rump. Many horses enjoy these new games and will follow you around to see what strange things you're going to do next. Curiosity is the opposite of fear, so be sure you always encourage and reward his curiosity, even if it's inconvenient for you.

Stand the mattress up against the fence. Touch and rub your horse with the plastic bag, then drape it over his back and ask him to walk around the pen. You have two goals: The first is to have your horse thoroughly understand and accept the nonthreatening aspects of these common objects, no matter how they might move or change shape, and the second is to let him know that he can *always* trust you when you ask him to accept strange new items and situations.

Next, introduce a new set of objects that can move or change shape or make noise. Some suggestions:

- Bring in a lawnmower, golf cart, or bicycle. (But keep your horse on a lead rope for these items, and don't let him stick a foot through the spokes or paw at the lawnmower to satisfy his curiosity.) Ask a friend to wheel the bicycle around the pen while you and your horse follow, then turn around and have the bicyclist follow your horse at a safe distance. Start the lawnmower or golf cart while your horse watches from a distance, then have a helper drive it around, a little closer each time, while you and the horse watch and follow. Ask friends to drive trucks, cars, tractors, and motorcycles around the yard or the arena.

- Stand in the middle of the pen and open an umbrella. Close it and invite the horse to explore. Open it, close it, put it on the ground, or hold it high over your head. Then approach and see if you can hold it over *his* head. (A curious horse may raise his head and try to nibble on the umbrella; don't let him poke himself in the eye or nose.)

- Tie a goat or llama outside the round pen, and let your horse become thoroughly familiar with the unusual sights, sounds, and smells.

- Introduce dogs, music, drums, a tuba, noisy children splashing in a wading pool. Hold a party near the barn, and let your horses watch all the commotion. If it's close to fireworks season, light off some sparklers or fire a rifle several times at a safe distance, gradually moving a little closer.

- Wave a flag or two over your head, and practice your semaphore code while playing a few Sousa marches on your boom box.

When you're ready to venture farther afield, take your horse to visit a school bus yard or watch bulldozers at a construction site. Seek out natural obstacles, too: streams, ditches, mud puddles.

Remember to stage familiar things in unexpected places, as well. Ask a friend to simply sit in a lawn chair and read a book somewhere unusual—perhaps out on a trail or at the bottom of a field. A horse's distance vision isn't very acute, so he may spend quite a bit of time trying to figure out what that strange object is. Something that remains still and *doesn't* move or make noise can appear very threatening to a horse until he has figured out what it is. Horses at their first three-phase event seldom refuse the jumps on cross-country courses; instead, they spook at the jump judges sitting in lawn chairs nearby.

If you anticipate and then simulate the challenges you know your horse will face, you can build a relationship of trust and obedience because your horse will know that you're going to provide wise guidance when he has to deal with something new. That's the attitude you want to instill with these exercises.

Joe, a 3-year-old Quarter Horse, is comfortable wearing and stepping on a garden hose. He's had ropes, bags, and plastic tarps draped over him, and as far as he's concerned this is just one big bore. His owner, Bird McIver, lets him know she's pleased with his quiet acceptance.

Joe expresses a little concern about walking over the tarp because it rustles and moves around a bit when he steps on it. Bird is giving him a chance to stand still and examine it before asking him to walk across. She's standing well out of his way, and her body posture is calm and reassuring. She's demonstrating what she'd like him to do: stop and look down at the tarp so he won't try to rush across.

Start with a small piece of cloth or plastic placed overhead so it's not flapping, then gradually ask your horse to accept more of everything—more movement, more sounds, more touching or bumping. Joe has walked through this gateway a couple of times without concern, so Bird is now making the plastic rustle a bit to see if that bothers him. He's interested but not worried.

Motor vehicles of all types and bicycles shouldn't pose a problem if your horse has been properly introduced to them. Have a helper drive the vehicle slowly away while you and your horse follow, to prove it's not a predator.

Step Three

Now it's time to ask your horse to do more than just passively accept, approach, or follow strange objects. In this third step, you'll ask him to step on, over, between, or under various items.

Walking Over Obstacles and Surfaces

Begin with something simple, sturdy, quiet, and motionless, such as a sheet of plywood or a well-constructed dry bridge. Lead your horse up to it and allow him to examine it, then circle around and ask him to walk over it. Lead him on a short but loose rope, and proceed as if you expect him to step right on and over it. Let him put his head down and look at it. Don't stop and face him or pin him with your eyes, don't drag him forward by the lead rope, and don't hang onto his head.

Reward! Even if he gets only one foot on the bridge and then steps off sideways, that's a positive attempt and it deserves a positive response from you. If your horse has successfully dealt with all the objects presented in steps one and two, this should not present any problems for him. And if he already loads well in a trailer, he should be thoroughly accustomed to stepping on and off a platform.

If he manages to squirm sideways and avoid stepping on the bridge, get a bigger bridge or position it near a wall or fence line so he has less chance to squirm away. Carry your long stick, say "walk" firmly, and add a tap of the stick to his hindquarters to encourage forward motion if he seems reluctant.

After he's comfortable with a dry bridge, introduce a tarp or a sheet of plastic stretched on the ground and held in place with bricks or poles. When walking over the stationary tarp becomes a ho-hum experience, let the edges of the tarp move around a little. If the wind catches an edge and blows it toward your horse, will he accept that? If not, rub a small piece of tarp or plastic bag all over his body, and after he's comfortable with that, ask him to walk again over the rustling plastic.

Many horses who do just fine over plywood or plastic have a difficult time walking on a mattress. Stepping on a mattress requires real trust because that giving-way-underneath feeling invokes fears of having their feet trapped, and your horse knows with absolute conviction that if he can't flee, he's going to become some predator's lunch.

Before asking your horse to cross that squishy mattress, introduce a foam mattress pad that's an inch or two thick; sleeping bag pads used by campers work well. If your horse has accepted the plastic tarp, he should accept this half mattress without too much hesitation. Provide plenty of reassurance and rewards, and give him lots of time to become comfortable walking over the foam pad. Then move on to a proper mattress (but no box springs, please!).

Be careful not to get stepped on when leading your horse over these obstacles. Many horses are willing to trust their handlers only if they can step precisely where you're stepping—obviously, that's the safest place for them to put their feet. Unfortunately, they often try to step *right there* while you're still standing in that spot. Be ready to push yourself away from your horse by planting your elbow against his shoulder, or be prepared to step quickly to the side as he comes over. Your horse may also try to leap the whole obstacle, and if he does, he's likely to land on or very close to you. Don't punish this behavior—after all, he's trying his hardest to comply with your request without being eaten by the mattress monster—but do wear sturdy shoes and keep yourself safe. Reassure and reward him for any positive attempt, however wild and sudden, and continue working to reduce his anxiety.

Stepping Around and Through Things

Three recommended exercises:

1. Arrange several old tires on the ground with their sides touching and ask your horse to walk over them. (Start with one line of side-by-side tires if he's at all anxious.) If he steps carefully, he'll probably try to place his feet in the centers of the tires. If he's not quite sure where all his feet are, he'll trip over or step on a squishy tire. Either is fine, as long as stumbling or stepping on a tire doesn't cause him to panic. Your goal in this exercise is to get him to accept the look and feel of strange things under his feet, not necessarily to win the next trail horse championship.

2. Cloth and plastic things that blow and touch his body don't cause much concern for a horse who is accustomed to wearing a winter blanket or fly sheet, but it's good to go through these trust-building exercises anyway. Set up two jumps or place rails on the tops of barrels to create a chute approximately six to eight feet wide, then drape old bedsheets or sheets of plastic over the rails. Lead your horse through the chute and watch his reaction. If he's comfortable, make the chute a little narrower and allow the sheets to blow and touch his body as he goes through. If he shows concern, keep the chute wide and anchor the fabric so it doesn't startle him the first few times. If he's fine going forward, ask him to back in and out of the chute.

3. Scatter poles randomly on the ground in a clustered, pick-up-sticks fashion, and lead or ride your horse through the poles. Encourage him to walk slowly, put his head down, and pick up all his feet carefully.

Walking Under Things

Drape a tarp over the top of a gateway. Let your horse explore, touch, and sniff it, then lead him through several times. Change the appearance or height of the tarp until he's comfortable even when it brushes the top of his head or back. Let him watch you as you climb up a ladder or the fence to change its appearance, so he'll be less concerned about activity above his head. (Contrary to popular belief, horses *do* notice things above their heads. I once owned a horse who enjoyed watching airplanes and large birds fly by. A blimp once kept him entertained for an entire afternoon.)

Set up a shade awning, dining tent, or portable carport and park your horse under it. Give him food and water there and let him hang out until he's thoroughly comfortable with it. Let him watch as you take it down or set it up.

After you've introduced everything from the ground, you can repeat most of these same exercises under saddle. Introduce and familiarize your horse with *everything* that catches his attention and causes anxiety. Know which items cause your horse the most concern, escalate gradually, and reward every step forward.

Although many of these exercises seem fairly arbitrary—please do this because I say so—you'll find that they actually have many practical applications. A horse who will walk over a dry bridge, through a narrow chute made of plastic tarps, and under a low overhang should load easily into a trailer. Temporary stalls at horse shows often consist of tarps and awnings, so you are wise to introduce these at home before adding to the stress at an unfamiliar show ground. A horse who will step on a mattress should have little trouble with mud and swamp crossings. When a blue tarp blows off the neighbor's pickup truck as you're riding down the road, you'd probably like your horse to remain steady and calm. Combat training, presented in a logical, low-stress, reward-based program, will help you and your horse manage these situations and many more.

15

USING POSITIVE TRAINING TO FIND SOLUTIONS TO SIX COMMON PROBLEMS

The Purpose of These Exercises

These exercises provide solutions to six common problems in the horse-human relationship. In each case, we'll look at the problem from the horse's point of view and develop a solution based on the positive training qualities of trust, respect, and rewards. In all of these cases, the underlying issue is a lack of trust and respect on the part of the horse—essentially, he doesn't feel he can trust and rely on his human leader, so he must resort to his own devices to remain safe and comfortable. Building trust and respect is always the first step in positive training.

Note that all of these exercises involve optional food rewards. When you're seeking to extinguish a negative response and simultaneously encourage positive behaviors, you'll want to have as many tools as possible in your rewards toolbox.

1. Poor Manners During Saddling

Horses who fidget, pull back, nip, strike, or otherwise try to avoid saddling can be a real test of a rider's patience. In serious cases that involve biting and kicking, they can also be dangerous.

The Cause

Horses who object to being saddled have been hurt, and they're afraid of being hurt again. Even if you place the saddle with infinite care and never overtighten the girth, if your horse has *ever* been in pain because of an ill-fitting saddle, a rider who twists the saddle out of position, pokes the horse in the ribs when he's mounting, or thumps down on the horse's back, you've probably got a horse who tenses up at least a little every time the saddle comes near. He feels he's got to try to escape what he believes will hurt him. If he can't escape, he needs to defend himself.

Before you can help your horse learn better manners during saddling, you need to find out why he reacts the way he does. There are many reasons why the saddling procedure can hurt or make a horse think he's going to get hurt.

- The saddle doesn't fit properly. It may be too narrow or too wide, pinch his withers, make his shoulders sore, or put too much pressure on weak back muscles. Even treeless saddles and saddles with adjustable trees can cause serious problems. Ask a competent saddler to check the fit of the saddle.

- The rider is too heavy. A horse should not be asked to carry more than 20 percent of his own weight, including all tack (no more than 15 percent if the rider is a beginner). Horses' backs are not designed to carry heavy loads, and if the muscles and ligaments are not properly strengthened through consistent, correct work, serious soreness can result. Inexperienced, clumsy riders are harder for a horse to balance than experienced riders.

- The horse was girthed up too tightly and too quickly. By far, this is the most common reason for horses to fear and hate the saddling process. A young horse, especially, can be easily hurt by an overtight girth, as his still-growing breastbone is composed mostly of sensitive cartilage.

The Solution

After you've made sure the saddle fits correctly and you're not going to ask your horse to carry more weight than he can comfortably bear, begin by bringing the saddle into view and placing it where your horse can see it while you groom him. Keep all your movements reassuring and quiet. Don't use overly abrupt gestures or a loud voice, which would raise your horse's anxiety level and put him on alert for possible pain and punishment.

As you groom, stay alert for your horse's reactions to you and the saddle. If he's calm and relaxed, reward him with voice and touch to reinforce his relaxation. Finish grooming, then pick up the saddle pad and approach him. If he fusses and fidgets, hold the pad out for him to examine, then put it back on the rack and pick up a brush. Brush and talk to him, and tell him he's a good boy for standing still. Concentrate on brushing his saddle and girth area, then put your brush down. Rub a little, and press your arm against his girth while you watch his reaction. Pat, praise, and hand him a carrot.

Now place the saddle pad on his back, wait for him to settle and stop fidgeting (even if it takes several minutes), and reward him with pats and rubs and a kind voice. Follow the same procedure with the saddle: Approach and retreat a few times, pat and rub when he's calm, and then place the saddle on his back even if he's fidgeting.

Proceed calmly to fasten the girth only as tight as you need to keep the saddle in place. This means you should be able to easily slide your hand between the girth and the horse's barrel and even be able to pull the girth away a few inches. Do not tighten more than this until the horse is relaxed. Plan to tighten the girth in three stages; this is only stage one.

Reward your horse every time he stands quietly! Be patient—don't rush to get outside and climb on. It will take time to convince your horse that he can trust you.

If he's so defensive about the process that he's likely to kick or bite, you *must* correct that behavior. Be alert for his head swinging around, and try to catch him with an elbow in the muzzle. But do not yell, hit, yank on the girth, or do anything else to punish. Your goal in this correction is to let the horse think he punished himself by swinging his head around with teeth open—it was his own action that got him into trouble, not your reaction.

If he's likely to kick, stay well out of range of his hind feet. Carry a short stick in your back pocket or in your right hand, and have it ready to pop him on the hind leg, just above the hock, if he strikes. Again, don't yell or overreact; your correction must be simple, swift, clear, and *over with*. Then find a moment when he's standing quietly and *reward him* again.

Your attitude should convey three messages: I will not hurt you with the saddle or girth, so you can trust me; I'm pleased when you are calm and relaxed; and sorry, but I will *not* tolerate dangerous behavior.

Lead your horse out of the barn to the arena, and let him walk around a little before tightening the girth further. Do the warm-up exercises described in chapter 8 and *then* tighten the girth a notch. If your horse is tall, always use a mounting block to get on so you don't pull the saddle sideways against his withers. After you're safely settled in the saddle, let him stroll around for another minute and then check your girth a third time. Tighten it from the saddle if it seems a little loose, but again, don't overtighten. You should still be able to get your hand between the girth and the horse at the widest point of his barrel. Before galloping, jumping, or strenuous hill climbing, check the girth again.

Get in the habit of checking your girth frequently so you can tighten it gradually, and don't ever force the girth tighter if the horse is obviously in distress. Be especially careful with a girth that has elastic on both ends, as it can be very easy to overtighten.

If your saddle tends to slip back or your horse has flat withers, add a breastplate to help hold things in place. If you ride in a western saddle with a cinch that can't be tightened while mounted, dismount after your warm-up walk to check for snugness.

2. Difficulty Bridling

The Cause

If your horse raises his head, clenches his teeth, yanks his head away when you touch his ears, and generally tries to avoid being bridled, the cause is essentially the same as with poor manners during saddling: At some time he's become convinced that the bridling process will hurt, so he doesn't trust his human leader to keep him safe and pain-free. It's particularly hard to gain the trust of horses who have had their sensitive ears grabbed and twisted in an ear twitch, a once-common method of subduing a resistant horse during saddle breaking, shoeing, or veterinary attention when tranquilizers were hard to come by. (A proper twitch made from rope, aluminum, or chain and used correctly on the upper lip is very different from, and much more humane than, the brutal ear twitch, in which the sensitive ear is grabbed by hand and twisted downward to force the horse to stand still.)

Training a horse to politely lower his head, open his mouth, and accept the bridle is not hard, but it does require lots of patience and careful handling. Unfortunately, it's even easier to teach a horse to resent the bridle. All you have to do is bump the bit against his teeth, try to force his mouth open when he's not ready, and yell at him if he attempts to protect his sensitive muzzle and mouth.

The Solution

First, make sure your horse's teeth are in good condition and the bridle and bit both fit correctly. Schedule a dental exam if he hasn't had his teeth attended to for six months or more.

Then figure out the different parts of the problem. Does he raise his head too high? Then begin by asking your horse to lower his head at your request. You can use any one of a variety of signals, but be consistent with the signal and with the reward:

Apply a quiet, steady (but not hard) downward pull on the halter so he feels pressure on his poll, and say "down, please." He may raise his head a little, turn away, or ignore you, but eventually—through his usual trial-and-error process—he'll drop his head a little. The moment he drops it—even a little, even if it goes right back up again—reward with a pat, praise, and a food treat such as a carrot or a small bite of grain. Stay relaxed, and repeat until his response is prompt and consistent. (This may take 10 minutes or an hour, but it *will* happen.)

Is he unhappy about having his ears touched, even when he's not being bridled? If so, you'll need to work on that separately. Start by rubbing and scratching his neck, occasionally pausing to ask him to lower his head if he raises it. Resume rubbing his neck as you work your way slowly up toward his ears. Just as he's about to pull away, stop, praise him, and hand him a carrot; then resume the rubbing and touching. This requires a balance between persistence and approach-withdrawal; your hands are not going to go away, but you also are not going to lose your temper or force him to submit. Some horses respond well to touches from the back of the hand rather than the palm, perhaps because the back of your hand can't grab his ear. Continue with slow movements, rubs, touches, and treats until the ears are no longer an issue.

Then hold the top of the bridle in your right hand and the bit plus a small slice of carrot in your left hand, as if you were about to bridle him. Ask for the head to come down and instead of putting the bit in, maneuver a piece of carrot into his mouth. Do this several times until he shows no concern about the bit's proximity but looks instead for the carrot.

Finally, feed him the carrot and the bit. To slide the bit in correctly, slip your thumb or middle finger into his mouth just behind the front teeth and be absolutely sure you don't clank the bit on his teeth or jam it uncomfortably into his mouth. If managing the carrot and the bit is too awkward, smear a little molasses or corn syrup directly on the bit, let him sniff and lick it, and then slide the bit in.

You shouldn't have to use food rewards every time you bridle your horse, but it's important to replace your horse's anticipation of pain in his mouth with the anticipation of something pleasurable in his mouth, and in this case, food treats work especially well. Are you bribing him? No, because he only gets the reward when he gives the desired response.

3. Refusing to Stand Tied

The Cause

There are two reasons why a horse might pull back and try to break away from a tie rope or crossties, and each reason requires a different solution.

If your horse panics and pulls back violently to get free, he's frightened. The initial stimulus might be very mild—someone drops a bucket suddenly nearby, or you bump into him accidentally as you are trying to hoist the saddle onto his back—and his response may seem to be all out of proportion to the cause. However mild the incident that sets him off, your horse is rediscovering that he's trapped by the tie rope and *that* causes the panic. His response seems to be one of sudden realization: "Heaven help me! I'm caught, trapped, *can't get free!*" And backward he goes, ready to fight anything and do any damage to himself or others in his attempts to flee. Once he's broken free, this horse will stay in flight mode, often running until he feels it's safe enough to stop. This is a panicked horse.

The second reason a horse will try to break free is because he's tired of standing around, he knows he can break his tie rope because he's done it before, and he simply knows how strong he is. This horse generally won't try to get free while you're present, he won't go into a true panic, and after he's broken his tie rope, he'll usually just put his head down to eat grass or wander off to visit his buddies. This is a stubborn and determined horse.

The Solution

Once you've determined which horse you're dealing with, plan your strategy. For the panicked horse, the first step is to reduce his nervousness and fear of noises, bumps, and sudden movements. Review the exercises in chapters 1, 2, and 14 to give him more confidence, increase his trust in you, and reduce the number of frightening things that may set him off. While you're helping him learn how to handle scary stuff, don't tie or crosstie him tightly to anything. Restrain him by merely looping a lead rope over a fence rail or tree branch, or keep him in his stall while you groom and saddle him. This will help him avoid the trapped feeling he gets when he's tied tightly. Reward all calm, relaxed behavior, and be alert to provide reassurance if he becomes anxious.

After he's worked through the trust-building exercises, outfit him with a snug-fitting, unbreakable rope halter and an unbreakable nylon tie rope tied to the halter. Find a nice sturdy tree (not a fence post or anything else that might get pulled out of the ground) in a cleared, level area with no rocks or obstructions, and fasten an unbreakable, thick, stretchy, rubber, bungee-type strap around the tree about a foot higher than the horse's head. Make absolutely sure no other animals or people can get close to the horse; he doesn't have to be isolated, but you want to keep everyone safe. Tie the horse to the stretchy strap, keeping your tie rope no more than two feet long, and leave the horse there to think about things. You can groom him or leave him alone, but keep an eye on him. About every five minutes, walk back, pat him and praise him, and give him a treat if you like; then leave him alone again.

At some point, he'll probably discover he's tied (trapped!) and go into a panic, pulling back rather violently. However, because he's tied high and short to something that gives a little but won't let go, he should learn fairly quickly that he can't get free—and, more importantly, that it's okay to be tied because *nothing bad is happening to him.* As soon as he gives up and springs forward again, move in quietly with your rewards and kind words. Reassure him that it's okay to be tied, he'll get rewards if he can keep the panic under control, and you'll be there to help him. Do not yell, hit him, or punish him in any way—he's already punishing himself.

Use a similar technique with the determined, stubborn puller, but instead of the stretchy inner tube or rubber tie, use a solid, unyielding attachment. This horse needs to understand the very clear limit of the tie rope. When he decides he's bored and wants to pull back, stay out of his way but also reprimand him sharply with your voice. When he settles and steps forward, reward him just as you would with the panicky horse because your objective is always to look for and reward the positive behavior.

For either type of horse, you'll have to repeat this lesson several times. Be absolutely sure your horse will stand quietly at his special tree for an hour or more with normal barn activity happening around him before you test him at any other hitching post. When you do tie him at other locations, try to tie him high up somewhere that's a little out of the way of busy traffic, so he can watch safely from a distance and not become anxious about unfamiliar activity.

Also, be aware that your horse can injure his neck and back by pulling back sharply. Schedule a visit from your veterinarian or equine chiropractor to deal with the possible impact of this correction.

4. Refusing to Load in a Trailer

The Cause

There are two reasons for a horse not to load in a trailer at your request: He's been hurt or frightened in a trailer, or he's never been properly trained to load and travel in one. In either case, his natural suspicions take over and he sees absolutely no reason why he should step into a narrow, dark space.

A horse can have a bad experience in a trailer without his owner realizing it. If your horse loaded just fine the last time you hauled him but now he won't load, he probably had a bad ride last time and doesn't want to repeat the experience. Trailers have rougher suspensions than cars, and it's hard for a half-ton horse to balance his weight going around corners and during starts and stops. Many drivers don't realize they have to accelerate, brake, and turn much more gradually with a trailer than with a car or truck, and it's very easy to throw a horse off balance and leave him scared and scrambling.

The Solution

First, make sure your trailer is as safe and as comfortable as you can make it. Lay down rubber mats to provide secure footing. Make sure there's enough space and headroom so your horse can shift his weight on turns and spread his hind legs wide for balance. Provide enough light and air so it doesn't appear to be a dark, smelly, confining hole. Make sure that everything is in good repair for safe, secure travel and that you use a cautious, experienced driver who will negotiate turns, stops, and rough roads slowly and calmly.

The type of trailer you have doesn't matter as much as training your horse to load in *any* trailer. Some horses are more accustomed to loading in step-up trailers than trailers with ramps, or vice versa. Horse owners in the eastern United States tend to prefer ramp-load trailers, saying that their horses feel better not having to step backward off a high step. In the western United States, people prefer step-up trailers so their horses can't slip sideways off a ramp as they unload. Many people like a slant-load trailer better than a straight-load trailer, claiming that the horse can keep his balance better in a slant-load trailer. An added advantage is that all but the very largest horses can turn around in a slant-load trailer to unload headfirst.

Whatever the style of trailer or the reason why your horse won't load willingly, the training process is the same. Expect to spend at least an hour on the first session, so set aside plenty of time, and don't let yourself be rushed. If you have success in less than an hour, great! If it takes two or three hours, then that's what it takes. You're going to persevere, regardless, and you are never going to lose your patience or hurt the horse. (Note that this is a training process, *not a gotta-get-him-on-it's-getting-dark solution. That's covered next.)

Next, confirm your horse's basic obedience on the ground. Review the exercises in chapters 6 and 7 to be sure your horse walks forward promptly, halts, backs, and shifts his hindquarters or shoulders at your direction. Go through the combat training exercises in chapter 14 to be sure your horse will walk under, on, and over anything you ask him to. (If he's fine with that, training a green horse to load in a trailer will be easy because he will trust you and the trailer won't stir up any negative memories.)

Then put a food treat in the front of the trailer so he can find it as soon as he gets in. Open all the doors and windows to make it as bright as possible. Put the halter, a long thick lead rope, shipping boots, and a helmet on your horse; put gloves on your hands, tuck a supply of food treats in your belt pack, pick up a long stick (a dressage whip or longe whip with the lash secured so it doesn't dangle or fly around), and lead your horse up to the trailer.

Don't ask him to load yet. Ask him instead to walk up to the trailer, stop about six feet away (closer if he's willing), and just *look* at it. Back up a few steps, turn, and walk up to the trailer again in a different place. Stop, turn, back up, walk forward, approach the trailer from a different angle, and repeat. For every correct response, reward! Rub his forehead or withers, talk to him, give him an occasional carrot. Rubs and talking will help reduce his anxiety because he knows he's pleasing you.

If he's reluctant to step forward at all, reach behind you with the whip and tap his hindquarters. If a single tap doesn't work, don't hit harder but do keep tapping, gently but firmly, until he moves up. If he pulls away and starts hauling you around where *he* wants to go, stop immediately and add a chain lead shank in the over-the-nose position shown in the photo on page 73.

Your simple goal is to establish your leadership and control in the presence of the dreaded trailer monster. Every time you ask him to walk forward, back up, and so on, you're demonstrating to him that he's safe because he's listening to you. (If he doesn't listen to you, you'll make him a little uncomfortable with the stick or the chain lead—but the *moment* he obeys, and *every time* he obeys, you must reward him *instantly* with praise and a forehead rub or a withers scratch and an occasional carrot.)

Keep doing this until you see signs of relaxation: lowered head, relaxed eyes and ears, and a general expression of bored acceptance. Then, using the same approach (walk, halt, back, halt, walk, halt, with lots of praise and reinforcement), walk to the back of the trailer, step into the trailer, and invite him to sniff and examine the inside. Stand to the side in a relaxed posture and don't stare him in the face. If he lowers his head to check things out, praise and reward. If he raises his head and appears alarmed but doesn't try to back away, praise and reward and wait. If he offers to step onto the ramp or into the trailer, praise a lot and reward!

Then ask him to back out, turn, walk, halt, back, walk, and approach the trailer again. This time ask him to keep walking forward as you walk right in. Don't turn around and stare at him, but be aware of what he's doing. If he hesitates, pay out a little line and take another step forward, asking him to take another step. If he hops in after you or makes any attempt to come forward, praise and reward, let him settle if he will, then tell him to back out again. If he goes forward and then loses his nerve and shoots backward, *don't* hang on his head or punish in any way. Just go with him, and as soon as he's clear of the trailer, ask him to walk forward a step or two and then halt. Repeat the entire procedure as many times as it takes, reinforcing your control on the ground outside the trailer and then asking him to walk into the trailer.

Eventually, he'll go in with all four feet and may even be willing to stand there as he explores the feed tub. Wonderful! But do *not* rush back to close up the tailgate. Instead, let him stand for a few minutes as you praise and reward and then ask him to back out. If he looks like he's made up his mind to back out before you give the command, *immediately* tell him to back so you can associate your command with his action. Walk him in and out a few times more, then put him away for the day.

The next day repeat the entire process, but you should be able to move on a little more quickly to the actual loading. If he's willing to stand quietly inside the trailer, have a helper close the tailgate or put up the butt bar while you stay in the trailer with your horse. Let him shift back, feel the confinement of the tailgate, repeat your command to halt, reward him, and just wait quietly until he settles. Then have your helper undo the tailgate. Wait a minute, reward the horse for standing quietly, then ask him to back out quietly. And reward him after he's out!

If he rushes, don't try to hold him or slow him down. If you hang on the lead rope, all you'll do is trigger the flight-or-fight response and he'll panic and maybe rear, hitting his head and becoming *convinced* that he shouldn't go in there. The only way to teach him to back out calmly is to give him lots of time and opportunities to practice backing out. As soon as he's safely out, reward him, let him settle, and repeat the exercise a few more times.

During the third session, you should be able to close the tailgate and take him for a slow, short, sedate ride. If he has a favorite buddy, bring the buddy along for companionship and reassurance—but be sure the buddy loads and travels well!

Leading Your Horse in Versus Self-Loading

Many people do not want to have to lead their horse into a trailer; rather, they want their horse to self-load. This is a handy skill, obviously, because if your trailer doesn't have an escape hatch or you're loading and hauling all by yourself, you'd like the horse to go in by himself so you can easily fasten the butt bar without having to climb around him to get out. Horses *should* be able to be managed both from the front (the human leads the horse) and the rear (the human drives the horse forward), but the reality is this: When you're dealing with a horse who has been hurt or frightened in a trailer, it doesn't make sense for the horse to step up into the trailer ahead of you. If you won't step into that scary place, why should he?

Don't push for self-loading too early. If he'll willingly follow you in but isn't confident enough to load on his own, that's okay. It may take a long time (and many good experiences to overcome the bad ones) to get your horse to self-load. The important thing is to get him feeling comfortable loading and traveling in the trailer, whether he goes in first or you do.

The Gotta-Get-Him-in-Now Solution

Sometimes you discover the problem too late, or you've just purchased a horse and didn't know he had a problem with trailers, or there's a medical emergency and you've got to help a friend load her horse *now*. First, try to park the trailer so there's a fence or natural barrier of some sort on one side, and tap the horse with a stick or whip as described on page 158.

If the tapping stick doesn't work to send the horse forward, drop the stick and get a longe line or a long rope. Have two trustworthy people (preferably wearing gloves so they don't get rope burns) bring the longe line up against the horse's butt, halfway between the tail and hocks, and use this as a come-along to boost him in. Don't let anyone get within kicking range of his hind legs, however, because a few horses will react to this method by letting fly with their heels in a spectacular show of mistrust. Two longe lines crossed behind the horse's butt will give you even more leverage.

If you don't have a longe line or the people to handle it, try a chain lead under the horse's chin. Run it through the left-hand halter ring and attach it to the right ring. Spend a few minutes getting the horse used to this—walk, halt, back, walk—and see how much pressure you need to apply to get the desired response. (If he's ridden in a pelham, kimberwicke, or curb bit, he's probably accustomed to some pressure under his chin. If he's never felt a curb chain before, he may be extremely sensitive to this pressure. Be as gentle as you can and only as firm as you need to be!)

Then ask him to load by applying slight, steady pressure on the chain. When he steps forward, release the pressure immediately. If he steps back, stay steady and let *him* increase the pressure. When he comes forward, relax and reward. Be careful with this method, as the chain under the chin can provoke him to rear. Don't let him hit his head or thrash anywhere near the trailer. Your goal is to make his life uncomfortable outside the trailer and whenever he backs away from it, while showing him that approaching and climbing into the trailer guarantees your approval and removes the pressure.

In this case, you'll want to close the tailgate as soon as you get him in. The proper training process will have to wait until later.

Problems Traveling in the Trailer

If your horse paws, kicks, or scrambles in the trailer while you're hauling, he's demonstrating his concern about something that's happening while the trailer is under way. If you don't fix the problem, he's going to become increasingly reluctant to load. Possible causes and solutions:

- An unfriendly companion. Make sure all horses are secured or separated so they can't nip or threaten other horses. A friendly buddy can be a big help for an anxious horse, but an unfriendly one can make the ride very unpleasant.

- Poor driving. If your horse scrambles or bangs on corners and curves, slow down! Trailers sway and whip around corners if you drive too fast, and your poor horse has no way of preparing for a sudden change in balance. You get to wear a seat belt, but he doesn't.

- The trailer is too narrow or too small. If he can't spread his legs to brace himself, he's going to feel like he's falling over, and he'll start kicking or scrambling. Give him room to balance.

- The horse hasn't had enough experience traveling and finding his balance. He simply doesn't know what to expect, so he gets anxious and paws or shifts his balance a lot. Take a few short, slow, no-pressure rides around the neighborhood with an amiable stablemate before you ask him to travel a long distance.

- Anticipating unloading. If your horse starts pawing every time your trailer stops in traffic, he's probably expecting you to open the doors and let him out. When you do get to your destination, don't hurry to let him out. Instead, feed him in the trailer, open a window, and let him look around, but ask him to spend a few minutes just standing there. Reprimand him for pawing, and praise him when he stands still.

5. Spookiness

The Cause

Spookiness in general demonstrates a lack of respect for and trust in the rider. The horse doesn't feel he can rely on his rider to tell him what to do or to keep him safe, so he goes into a hyperalert state to keep himself safe from real or imagined dangers. However, there can be several underlying causes:

- Your horse might be truly fearful in an unfamiliar setting, such as when a young horse goes to his first show and feels that *everything in the universe* is outside his comfort zone.

- Your horse has too much energy. He can't pay attention until he's met his basic needs to blow off steam and *move*, so he'll spook even at familiar objects because they give him a chance to move.

- Your horse is cold. When temperatures plummet, his feet hurt, his skin tingles, and his response is to move in any way possible to relieve that tension. If he's cold and stiff, his ability to flee from predators is compromised, and that also makes him more fearful in general.

- Your horse has decided it's just too much work, and he doesn't believe his rider has enough authority to be in charge, so stopping and staring at something gives the horse a chance to challenge your authority.

The Solution

First, you must identify the cause and determine whether the horse is truly fearful or something else is happening. *Do not punish a fearful horse.* Work instead to develop his trust in you so that when you tell him it's safe to listen and obey, he'll believe you. Go through the obedience and trust building exercises in chapters 6 and 7 and the combat training exercises in chapter 14, and reward all your horse's attempts to be brave and follow your lead. Remember that lateral work will help you gain control over your horse's hindquarters, and leg-yielding can get your horse safely past many fear-inducing objects.

If he's simply got too much energy or must move vigorously to get warm, turn him out and let him run. You can work him down a little on the longe as well, but be careful of using the longe line to let him blow off steam. Longeing is training, and you don't want your horse to think that he can gallop wildly, buck, or kick on the longe.

Then get back on, work on exercises such as those in chapters 11 and 12 to help him develop his attention and balance, and praise his compliance and obedience whenever you get it. Keep him busy to help him focus, work on lateral work (especially leg-yielding), and provide lots of opportunities for him to succeed at being forward and obedient. After he's thoroughly warmed up, review some of the combat training exercises in chapter 14 to help develop his trust and respect.

Don't punish a spook. Instead, stay centered and immediately give him something to do to restore his focus on you. Leg-yielding, a turn on the forehand, a halt, a back—all these will remind him he needs to listen to you.

If your horse is slightly lethargic and seems to spook at things not out of fear but out of a determination to challenge your authority, go back to the basic stop-and-go exercises in chapter 11 to reinforce obedience. Use the combat training exercises in chapter 14 to help your horse understand that he needs to respect your authority and go forward when requested.

6. The Barn-Sour Horse

The Cause

The horse who always wants to leave the arena or run back to the barn, or who won't leave it in the first place, has serious issues with trust, security, and respect. He doesn't feel secure away from his barn or his buddies because he doesn't trust or respect you. You haven't convinced him that you're a worthy leader, so he doesn't feel he needs to do what you tell him.

The Solution

You need to establish control in his home territory before you try to take him anywhere else. If he won't go forward under saddle, he probably won't go forward very well when you're leading him, either. Work on the groundwork exercises in chapters 6 and 7, concentrating especially on anything that requires your horse to move forward promptly or to shift his body away from you at your command.

Don't let your horse's uncooperative attitude affect *your* attitude. You need to remain firm, calm, upbeat, and ready to reward even the slightest improvement in his respect for you. Make sure he's familiar with your approval voice and reward touches, not just your frustrated voice and angry hands. Your goal is to develop a cooperative, willing horse, not just to force him to grudgingly do your bidding.

Be very consistent! Don't reward for good behavior one day and then forget to reward the next day. Many balky horses get that way because they've never been clearly and consistently rewarded for doing something right, so they never get the reinforcement they need.

After you've established a pattern of prompt responses from the ground, in a place where your horse is willing to work, take him farther away—perhaps around to the back of the barn or on the far side of the arena where he can't see his buddies or his stall, someplace that's just a little outside his comfort zone. Carry your whip, and enforce forward by tapping on his hindquarters as you lead him. Don't allow any foot-dragging or sluggishness. He *must* march along promptly with no hesitation because *you* are the leader, not him. If he tugs away, add a chain leadshank and calmly remind him of his responsibility to listen to you.

Then go a little farther afield, still on foot, and repeat the same exercises. Find a problem area—perhaps he won't go down the trail alone, or into a lower pasture, or to the end of the driveway—and quietly insist on his obedience. Go through all your drills and exercises in many different places: walk, halt, back, walk, trot, stop, turn.

Then get on the horse, and work on the mounted exercises in chapter 11. Continue alternating the groundwork and mounted exercises, paying special attention to lateral exercises such as turns on the forehand and leg-yielding. And when you feel he's really listening, take him off down the trails or wherever you've had problems and allow him to relax. Your goal is to show him that when he listens to you, he can rest and receive a reward. Correct any disobedience firmly, but reward equally lavishly when he complies.

When it's time to head home, if he's inclined to rush back, hop off and lead him. Ask him to halt, back, turn, and so on, and then let him proceed toward home as a reward for good behavior.

This takes time and bushels of patience on your part, but in the end you'll have a horse who understands that you're the leader and that if he follows your lead, he'll be comfortable and well rewarded for his efforts.

EPILOGUE

This book and these exercises have been developed for two purposes:

1. To help riders become more attentive to the needs and motivations of their horses, so humans can give their horses what the horses want and need.

2. To promote the usefulness of our horses, so they can provide what we humans want and need.

When horses and humans are consistently rewarding each other through their actions and responses, there's harmony. And when a horse is more useful to humans, the horse will have a better life because people are more likely to treat him kindly and take good care of him.

The responsibility for training, teaching, and learning always rests with the humans, not the horses. Our horses don't have a "duty" to do what we say, and they have no concept of what is "right" or "wrong." They have only the logic of their instincts to tell them what brings pleasure or pain.

If we can always keep our horses' needs foremost, ahead of our own; if we can keep an open mind and recognize that learning to communicate with our horses is a never-ending process, not just an end product; and if we can find our own rewards in our horses' accomplishments and well-being—then we are worthy partners for our horses.

GLOSSARY

Bitless Bridle   Developed by Robert Cook, FRCVS, Ph.D., the Bitless Bridle communicates to the horse by applying pressure over the poll, under the jaw, and across the bridge of the horse's nose.

center of gravity   The dynamic point of physical equilibrium for horse or human. The center of gravity, or point of balance, changes as the activity changes. The faster your horse goes or the harder he accelerates, the farther forward his center of gravity shifts, and the farther forward your center of gravity must shift to remain in balance.

combat training   Also called bombproofing or spookproofing. The careful, controlled introduction of fearful situations and simulated dangers to help a horse become accustomed to strange objects, sounds, and movements. Properly structured combat training builds a horse's trust and reliance in his human leader.

comfort zone   Where a horse (or human) feels knowledgeable, confident, and safe. A newborn foal's comfort zone is no larger than his mother's shadow; an experienced parade horse's comfort zone will include marching bands, balloon vendors, and screaming children.

curb bit   A bit that applies leverage to the horse's bars, chin, and poll. Curb bits have shanks to which the reins are attached and a curb chain or strap that tightens under the horse's chin when pressure is applied. Curb bit mouthpieces may be jointed or unjointed, with or without a port. Kimberwickes count as mild curb bits, unless the reins are attached in such a way that they apply no pressure to the poll or the curb chain under the chin.

dressage   In French, *dressage* means "training and preparation." In current use, it refers to the systematic, gymnastic training of the horse to develop ever-increasing balance, impulsion, and collection. Developed originally by the ancient Greeks, dressage is one of the three classical equestrian competitions, along with show jumping and three-day eventing.

extinction   The pattern of learning (or unlearning) that occurs when no feedback is provided for a behavior. Never offering a reward for good behavior will cause the good behavior to be extinguished.

half-halt   Coordinated action of the legs, seat, and hands to improve the horse's attention and help him rebalance.

leg-yielding   A sideways-forward (lateral) movement in which the horse's body remains straight and his poll and jaw are slightly flexed away from the direction of movement. This is a good exercise to develop obedience and suppleness.

negative reinforcement   The pattern of learning that occurs when a negative stimulus (something uncomfortable or irritating) is removed. Release of pressure on the reins or halter when the horse halts correctly is an example of negative reinforcement.

positive reinforcement   The pattern of learning that occurs when a specific behavior receives a reward. The horse learns something new by associating a reward with a previously unrelated behavior. A rub on the withers for standing still and a carrot for stepping into a trailer are examples of positive reinforcement.

punishment   Also called correction. A pattern of learning that occurs when an undesirable behavior results in an immediate and undesirable consequence; for instance, when a high-ranking horse nips or kicks a lower-ranking horse for attempting to steal food.

reward cycle   The pattern of request-response-reward that effective trainers use to communicate with their horses. Rewards must always be clear, prompt, consistent, and appropriate to the task. In other words, a brand-new task requires a very clear request and a large reward; a more familiar task can be paired with a more subtle request and a smaller reward.

rewards toolbox   Whatever the trainer can use to reward the horse for correct behavior. Primary rewards include release of pressure, reduction of anxiety, increase in balance, comforting touch, rest, freedom, and food. Secondary rewards include the trainer's approval, removing threat gestures, and other neutral signals of approval or disapproval.

sliding sidereins   An auxiliary rein, used while riding, longeing, or driving, that can help a horse learn to accept light rein contact in a round, balanced frame. It attaches to the near side of the girth at its midpoint, passes through the nearside bit ring, between the horse's front legs and through a D-ring on the center of the girth, back up to the offside bit ring, and to the midpoint of the offside of the girth.

snaffle bit   A bit that works directly in the corners (lips) of the horse's mouth, without applying leverage pressure to the horse's chin or bars of the mouth. Snaffles may also apply pressure to the tongue, depending on the curve and shape of the mouthpiece. (One type of snaffle, a hanging or Baucher snaffle, also applies a small amount of pressure to the poll.) Snaffle bits may have unjointed, single-jointed, or double-jointed mouthpieces.

transition   A change in gait, or a change in the length of the stride within a gait. A good trainer prepares a horse for transitions by giving a small alert signal and then asking quietly for the change.

trust builder   Any experience that reinforces your horse's trust, confidence, and respect in his human leader.

trust buster   Any experience that destroys your horse's trust in you. A major trust buster occurs whenever your horse gets hurt or badly frightened as a result of your poor leadership decisions. Lesser trust busters include situations in which you fail to lead, fail to command respect, or fail to reward good behavior.

turn on the forehand   A lateral exercise in which the horse pivots his hindquarters around his forehand.

turn on the haunches   A lateral exercise in which the horse pivots his forequarters around his haunches (hindquarters).

REFERENCES

Bean, Heike, and Sarah Blanchard, *Carriage Driving: A Logical Approach to Training Through Dressage*, classic edition. Hoboken, N.J.: Howell Book House, 2004.

Bucklin, Gincy Self, *How Your Horse Wants You to Ride*. Hoboken, N.J.: Howell Book House, 2004.

———, *What Your Horse Wants You to Know*. Hoboken, N.J.: Howell Book House, 2003.

Cook, Robert, *The Bitless Bridle*^{TM} *by Dr. Robert Cook*. www.bitlessbridle.com.

Dawson, Jan, *Teaching Safe Horsemanship*, 2nd ed. North Adams, Mass.: Storey Publishing, 2003.

de Kunffy, Charles, *Training Strategies for Dressage Riders*, 2nd ed. Hoboken, N.J.: Howell Book House, 2003.

Gray, Lendon, *Lessons with Lendon*. Garthersburg, Md.: Primedia Equine Network, 2003.

Maslow, Abraham, *Motivation and Personality*, 2nd ed. New York: Harper & Row, 1970.

Podhajsky, Alois, *My Horses, My Teachers*. New York: J. A. Allen & Co., 1977.

Savoie, Jane, *Cross-Train Your Horse*. North Pomfret, Vt.: Trafalgar Square Publishing, 1998.

Schaffer, Michael, *Right from the Start: Create a Sane, Soft, Well-Balanced Horse*. North Pomfret, Vt.: Trafalgar Square Publishing, 2002.

Shrake, Richard, *Resistance Free Training*. North Pomfret, Vt.: Trafalgar Square Publishing, 2000.

Tellington-Jones, Linda, *An Introduction to the Tellington-Jones Equine Awareness Method: The TEAM Approach to Problem-Free Training*. Sharon Hill, Pa.: Breakthrough Publications, 1988.

INDEX

ABOUT THE AUTHOR

SARAH BLANCHARD is a professional horse trainer and riding instructor with more than 40 years of teaching experience. She began riding "too far back to remember" at her family's boarding stable in Stamford, Connecticut. Her mother provided early riding lessons on a series of challenging ponies, while her father, a dairy farmer, taught her to hitch and handle driving horses.

As a teenager, Sarah polished her skills in hunt seat equitation under the eye of well-known trainer Victor Hugo-Vidal, Jr., and competed in AHSA Medal and Maclay hunt seat equitation classes. She was also active for many years in the 4-H Club, representing Connecticut in a regional hunt seat competition at the Eastern States Exposition. After the family farm was sold, Sarah spent several summers teaching riding and jumping at camps in New Hampshire and New York.

At the University of Connecticut, Sarah was active in both the liberal arts and animal science programs. She was also a member of UConn's Intercollegiate Horse Judging Team, which placed second at the national finals in 1971. She also competed in UConn's Little International Horse Show, winning the hunt seat equitation championship three years in a row.

After college, Sarah established a small stable in northeastern Connecticut, where she taught riding for many years and was active in the Tri-State Horseman's Association. She was also one of the founders of the well-known Pomfret, Connecticut, Hunter Pace, which draws hundreds of horses and riders from throughout New England.

After developing an interest in dressage and combined training, Sarah competed her homebred Appaloosa-Thoroughbred gelding, Cuhoolain, at many events throughout southern New England, qualifying for the Area I Training Level championship in 1990.

Sarah is a licensed instructor in Massachusetts, where she lived for several years. As an adviser to the Eye of the Storm Equine Rescue Center in Stow, Massachusetts, she helped evaluate and rehabilitate neglected and abused horses and also worked as a volunteer fund-raiser. A popular trainer, clinician, and judge, Sarah has judged local and 4-H Club shows in New York, Connecticut, Massachusetts, Rhode Island, Vermont, and Hawaii, where she now lives with her husband, two Miniature Schnauzers, a calico cat, and a former steeplechaser from New Zealand who is finding a new career as a lesson horse.

Since moving to Hawaii, Sarah has become a popular clinician and instructor in dressage and jumping. She serves on the board of directors of the Hawaii Isle Dressage and Combined Training Association and is chair of the Panaewa Equestrian Center Development Group, where she works with local residents and county officials to expand the equestrian opportunities on the island. She teaches business writing at the University of Hawaii in Hilo. Her articles have been published in *Equus*, *Dressage and Combined Training*, *Horse Illustrated*, and *Horseman's Yankee Pedlar*.

Sarah has also leased the Quarterhorse mare Coosa Lani, who appears in many of the photos in this book. Coosa Lani is bred to a Belgian warmblood stallion for an August 2005 foal. Sarah's present focus in riding is to improve her skills in classical dressage; she is currently riding in clinics with Germany's well-known international trainer and judge, Alex Wortmann.

Along with her work with horses, Sarah found the time to earn her MBA. Twenty years in corporate marketing, plus her college teaching experience, have contributed to many of the insights described in *The Power of Positive Horse Training*.

"Everything we learn from horses can help us understand people and vice versa," Sarah explains. "Underlying motivation, rewards, the need for approval from the leader—whether you're dealing with horses or humans, it's very similar. The difficult part is getting the communication right, translating from horse to human and back again. That's my goal: to make the horse-human communication as clear and easy as possible, so both the horses and the humans receive the rewards and learn to work together in harmony."